Smiles and Tears

Archie Smith

Tales worth telling

from

Gorran and beyond

Front cover - *From a painting by Ernest Oliver showing Beach Corner, Rock Beach and the old village, viewed from the Pound. Although contemporary it recaptures the atmosphere of this one-time isolated village*

Smiles and Tears

Copyright © Archie Smith 1998

All rights reserved. No part of this publication may be reproduced or transmitted in any form or by any means, electronic or mechanical, including photocopy, recorded or any information storage and retrieval system, without the permission in writing from the author.

ISBN 1 897745 07 9

Published by CAMOMILE PRESS, 'Claybourne', Stenalees, St. Austell, Cornwall PL26 8ST
Printed by *SwiftPrint*, Carclaze, St. Austell, Cornwall PL25 4EW
August 1998

Chapters

INTRODUCTION.	1
WHERE DO YOU COME FROM?	2
GORRAN HAVEN QUAY	3
THE CHINA CLAY FIGHT	7
FISH IN PLENTY	15
THE SMITH CONNECTION WITH GORRAN	17
LISTENING FOR 'TICKERS'	19
THE QUEST FOR FRUITS DE MER ON THE SEASHORE	20
THOUGHTLESSNESS - A SOBERING RESULT	21
BODRUGAN BROAD LANE	23
GORRAN AND CRICKET	24
THE BILLING FAMILY	28
HEAVEN ON EARTH BY THE SEA	31
THOMAS SANDERS AND THE SHIP INN	35
THE WRECK OF THE 'SHIP'?	36
A SOBERING REMINDER.	38
AN EXAMPLE TO FOLLOW: A LESSON TO REMEMBER	41
PICTURES	43 - 68
A SENSE OF HUMOUR	69
A CORNISH INVOLVEMENT IN THE BOER WAR, 1899	72
THE CRUEL SEA	74
BRAVERY ON THE DEADMAN AT DEAD OF NIGHT	75
A NAVAL TRAGEDY, 100 YEARS AGO.	79
THE DODMAN CROSS	82
THE LOSS OF THE ARDANGORM.	84
WORLD WAR TWO - FORCES' KILLED, GORRAN PARISH	88
IN FLANDERS FIELDS THEY LIE TOGETHER	91
THE OLIVERS.	94
LANHYDROCK AND THE NATIONAL TRUST	98
DO NOT STAND AT MY GRAVE AND WEEP.	102
GLOSSARY OF DIALECT WORDS USED IN GORRAN PARISH.	104

THE AUTHOR

"Archie Smith lives in Gorran Haven where his forebears have lived for centuries and where he spent his boyhood.
He became a schoolmaster, and spent most of his career teaching at two St. Austell Secondary schools, periods which gave him much pleasure whilst allowing him to remain in his own village and pursue the local way of life so dear to him.
In 1992 he wrote the story of his youth between the two world wars, and the book 'Laughs and Sweet Memories' was widely acclaimed as a valuable piece of social history and a nostalgic 'trip' for Cornish people everywhere.
Although he claims to be no writer, historian or raconteur, and to have the schoolmasters' scant sense of humour, few of his readers or those who know him would agree."

Other books by this author

Laughs and Sweet Memories,	ISBN 1 897745 00 1	1992
Uphill All The Way	ISBN 1 897745 02 8	1994
To Commemorate 100 years of Gorran Parish Council	ISBN 1 897745 03 6	1994

INTRODUCTION

This little book is a miscellany of true stories and historical vignettes associated with Gorran Haven, the parish of Gorran and the southern part of Mid Cornwall.
It is entitled "Smiles and Tears" because it contains not only little articles, which may bring smiles to the faces of its readers, but also stories, which should cause them to reflect deeply.
There are, therefore, stories of events, of people, of life as well as personal comments.
So "Smiles and Tears" - and that sums up life in three words as well as the contents of the book!

Archie Smith
1998

"My people didn't come over with the Phoenicians: we were here to greet them." (An Gof)

WHERE DO YOU COME FROM?

This is a question asked frequently of visitors wherever they are. If it is posed to me, the answer will depend on where I am. If I am abroad, the answer will be "England". If I am in England, the answer will be "Cornwall", and if I'm in Cornwall, the answer will be "Gorran". So I am English when abroad, Cornish when in England and "a Gorran man" when in the County.

But what is it to be Cornish? Is it through birth, ancestry, claim, adoption or accent?

I have no problem, because my ancestors, both paternal and maternal, have lived in the parish of Gorran for at least three hundred years: I speak the dialect, I retain my Cornish accent and I am at home with Cornish people. Yet in spite of this, a fiercely Cornish Nationalist, whatever that means, once accused me of "being Anglicised up to my eyeballs". I was amused, and still laugh when it comes to mind!

If you listen to people talking throughout Cornwall, you will soon realise that there are people with backgrounds and accents from every part of the United Kingdom. They live among us and mainly through choice: they have adopted us, in one sense.

In my own village of Gorran Haven, there is less than one in forty over the age of fifty who was born and bred here, and it is not unusual for one of the thirty-nine to ask me where I came from. This is somewhat amusing and a little hurtful, but these newcomers often run our communities. In my Parish, those who have come to live here because of their love of all that we have to offer, seek to show their appreciation by service to us.

The Parish of Gorran is but one of many in Central and East Cornwall where community life would be much poorer but for the incomers. So are they Cornish? I think not, nor would they claim or probably wish to be.

But to me, these good people are not strangers nor foreigners but true parishioners: I say to each, "You'm wan o'we," or, being interpreted, "You are one of us," - and there is no greater compliment than that.

'Safe into the haven guide' (Charles Wesley)

GORRAN HAVEN QUAY

Records of a sea fishery at Gorran Haven date back to 1270 and the Taxation of 1271 (which dealt with tithes) refers to seines, one of the earliest references to seining in the country, and shows that pilchard fishing was of prime importance even then.

In 1570 came the first actual record of the fishing community in Gorran Haven and 68 men were listed. Mevagissey had but 8.

In 1894 the Merchant Shipping Act required fishing boats to be registered, and Fowey's register between 1902 and 1907 contains particulars of 200 boats. Of these, 70 belonged to Mevagissey, 57 to Looe, 43 to Gorran Haven and 1 to Portloe.

Boats need protection unless sheltered from all winds, and as Gorran Haven is especially vulnerable to all winds from N.N.E. to S.S.E. and Southerly too, a quay was vital and was always seen to be. It is thought that up to six quays have been built at Gorran Haven over the centuries. and most were washed away by heavy gales or through lack of maintenance.

From at least 1840 to 1886 there was no quay and this brought serious consequences. Not only were the fishermen faced with the back-breaking job of hauling their boats up and down when the weather threatened, but also the property in the immediate vicinity of the shore suffered serious damage. On January 2nd, 1867, a severe gale from the East washed away part of the Ship Inn near Beach Corner and other properties also sustained serious damage.

But help was to come. In 1852 the Caerhays estate was purchased from the Trevanions by the Williams family who had made their fortune from mining. The Bodrugans had backed Richard III at Bosworth Field in 1485, and the Trevanions had benefited from their downfall, building among others, a huge mansion at Caerhays and extending it in the 1750s. But they 'overdid it', and as they were inveterate gamblers too, their properties had to be mortgaged and eventually sold.

The present castle at Caerhays was restored by John Charles Williams, a kindly and generous man, whose estate now included the land to the South of the stream running down to the beach. However, the quay and pound area belonged to the Duchy of Cornwall from whom Mr. Williams purchased it for the sum of £5. He decided to build a quay for the fishermen of Gorran Haven and this he did at a cost of several thousand pounds: it was completed in November, 1886.

In 1917, the fishermen formed a Co-op, the capital for it coming from the fishermen who bought shares at £1 each. Most, in fact, bought about twenty. The Co-op thrived. It assumed responsibility for the maintenance of the quay and the pound and became a trading station in several ways. The sale of all fish (especially shell-fish) was organised, a lorry was purchased for its transport to St. Austell station, fishing gear and clothing for the fishermen too were bought and sold to them at cost price: all augured well.

The outbreak of the war in 1939 signalled the beginning of the end of Gorran Haven as a real fishing village. Young men were called up for the forces, leaving only the old ones to continue, but already these young men had begun to turn their backs on fishing as a livelihood, encouraged to do so by their fathers who could scarcely earn a living from it.

In the 1950s but a few full-time fishermen remained and it became abundantly clear to them that they could not keep the Co-op going. The lorry was sold, the lorry store too, the packing shed was closed - it was the end. But that responsibility for the repair and maintenance of the quay remained.

1961 was a critical year. In the spring, a very severe North East gale had swept huge seas around the Northern end of the quay and across the harbour, pounding the deck mercilessly where the quay widens. The damage done was alarming. The deck was torn off, the apron, i.e. the foundation near the quay's end was undermined, and in danger of collapsing. The foreshore from Beach Corner to Fort was badly eroded causing danger of cliff falls, and the sewage pipe at the back of the quay had its concrete covering torn off. Pipe fractures caused raw sewage to spew out everywhere: urgent action was needed all round.

The fishermen were faced with an impossible situation. The cliff was the responsibility of the Rural District Council as was the sewage pipe, but the quay was theirs. They had but slender funds; they had to look for help. Their Chairman, Bill Hammond and Secretary Spencer Holland, had contacted all the possible sources of help but they were given only excuses which amounted to refusals. The Ministry would only help if there was a Harbour Board, and there was none. The Chairman of the Parish Council, Robert Wellington, accompanied by fishermen's representatives Lewis Billing and Jim Liddicoat addressed the full rural District Council and pleaded their cause with no success. The Cornwall Sea Fisheries Committee had to consider in due time. In view of the urgency of repairs, Robert Wellington and Wally Sabey, our R.D.C. councillor, called a public meeting at the Institute to urge the setting-up of a fund to save the quay. On September 24th 1962 local contributions had reached a total of £782. Meanwhile, a Harbour Board had been formed, and in consequence, the Ministry of Agriculture and Fisheries had donated £1500. By January, 1964, the quay had been repaired, all bills paid, and a total of £462-16-2 remained in hand. This was deposited in Lloyd's Bank, 'to be used when all other funds had been exhausted' and was to be known as 'the Quay Fund'.

In 1968 the Parish Council decided that as the Chairman was a Trustee of the Quay Fund, the Parish Council had an interest in the quay; and began an unsuccessful search for the deeds. What a muddle it all was!

The 'Harbour Board', the few fishermen still trying to earn a living and 'keep things going', were in no financial position to do so. Moreover, aware of their responsibility to maintain and repair the quay, they realised their position was desperate; what could they do?

At a final meeting it was unanimously agreed to approach 'the Judge' for advice. This was Mr. Hugh Park, a distinguished Q.C., who had first come to Gorran Haven in 1946. A life-long lover of the sea and a keen fisherman too, he fell for the Haven's charm, bought a Cottage near the harbour, acquired a boat and come down whenever he could get away. But not only so; he was friendly, interested in the fishermen, their work and their affairs. So Lewis Billing and 'Boy Jim' Liddicoat explained their dilemma to him and looked at him eagerly for his reaction. "I'll see into it for you," he replied, and the word went round. "The Judge is going to see to it for us."

Mr. Justice Park (now Sir Hugh) enlisted two other men, Mr. Frank Brown and Mr. Douglas Marr. Frank, the grandson of a Post Office official who retired to Gorran Haven for health reasons in 1908, had never lived in the village but had never ceased to visit whenever he could and shared the same interest as Sir Hugh. A successful business-man of wide experience and with a generous nature, his help would be invaluable. And to complement these, Douglas Marr, a renowned City solicitor and another keen sailor made up a most able trio. Suffice it to state that all the papers associated with the Co-op, the Pound and the background to the quay were gathered and collated. The ownership of the quay and the pound was established and the boundaries delineated. In fact, the fishermen owned the freehold of the quay and the pound, together with that part of the beach between the Northern end of the pound wall and the Northern end of the quay. The Gorran Haven Harbour and Fishermen's Society was born and every step was taken to set it up on a sound, secure and inviolable legal basis. The responsibilities of the old Harbour Board (i.e. the repair and maintenance of the quay) were subsumed, mooring and pound fees were introduced to afford financial viability, and the Society was away! The control and administration of the harbour is carried out by a management committee elected by members at each Annual General Meeting and applicants for membership of the Society are considered each year and elected by secret ballot.

THE GORRAN HAVEN HARBOUR AND FISHERMEN'S SOCIETY IS A de facto 'QUAY PRESERVATION SOCIETY'

South West Water have been granted a 99 year lease at a satisfactory annual rental reviewable every three years for the Sewage Pumping Station in the pound, and the Trustees of the 'Quay Repair Fund' have released the money accrued - now over £4,300 - which is being covered pound for pound by the Society for a special repair fund.

The Society engages highly qualified surveyors to make a detailed structural survey of the quay every three years, and their report is, and will be, acted on immediately. Moreover, Mr. Chris Lobb has kindly made a detailed analysis of the quay's deck, and a plan has been formulated to gradually replace worn coping stones and the unsuitable concrete repairs with cobbles in an effort to bring the quay up to its original condition. It is hoped that this aim will be realised in the year 2000!

'Here I stand' (Luther)

THE CHINA CLAY FIGHT

There is no doubt that the greatest perceived threat to the future of Gorran Haven was launched by the China Clay companies in October, 1969 when they published detailed proposals to pump all their micaceous residue to an outfall about 800 yards off Penamaen (or Maenease) Point.

A full report on the ensuing events which lasted nearly two years would fill a book, and perhaps that is an exercise which someone may undertake in the future. The papers detailing their two year fight, fought relentlessly by the locals, have been lodged with the County Archivist at County Hall.

Suffice it, therefore for me to publish three distinct aspects:

a) the fishermen's deposition when shown the plans;

b) the Residents' Association's statement re the proposals, and

c) the result.

N.B. Over 2,000 of the Residents' Association's statements were produced and published nation-wide within three weeks of the proposals being made public. The statement was never challenged.

(a) **We, the undersigned, being life-long fishermen of Gorran Haven have been informed of the proposals of the China Clay Association to dispose of micaceous waste into the sea half a mile off-shore from Maenease Point.**

We have further been informed of the estimated quantity of material to be so pumped into the sea during the next 60 years i.e. 200,000,000 tons.

We have also examined the map showing the position of the outfall pipe and the area estimated to be eventually covered by this waste material.

It is our considered opinion and we are unanimous that:-

1. This effluent will gradually extend over a much wider area than that

shown on the map by the combination of tide and wind, causing extensive contamination of the sea bed and seriously affecting some of our best shell fishing grounds. This area would extend into the Mevagissey Bay to the East and into the Veryan Bay to the West and obliterating eventually the well known and prolific Dodman fishing grounds.

2. The coastline and beaches to the West as far as Caerhayes, Portholland, Portloe and Portscatho would be affected and to the East the Gorran Haven and Perhaver beaches eventually reaching beyond Chapel Point.

3. On account of the severe Easterly and South-Easterly gales which persist for several weeks each year quantities of this waste would be stirred up in this fairly shallow water and deposited on the foreshore, particularly at Vault and Gorran Haven.

4. When a gale coincides with the peak of a high spring tide the movement of the waste would be considerable.

5. White water would be visible over a much larger area than that mentioned in the report.

Signed	W. Ball, Gorran Haven
Signed	L. Billing, Gorran Haven
Signed	J. Liddicoat, Gorran Haven
Signed	M. J. Patten, Gorran Haven
Signed	H. Johns, Gorran Haven
Signed	A. W. Pollard, Gorran Haven
Signed	J. F. Guy, Gorran Haven
Signed	M. V. Guy, Gorran Haven

(b)   **Gorran and District Residents' Association Statement re: China Clay Association Proposals.**

The effluent from the China Clay Industry which is milky white in colour, is mainly a micaceous residue carried in suspension in water. When this residue is deposited on the sea or river bed it forms a soft sticky layer which may not only smother all life beneath it, but discourages life above it. This will most certainly continue whilst the deposit is in a state of agitation.

Since China clay mining began in the 18th century the effluent has been disposed of through the rivers in the area, the Winnick (known as the White River), the Par River and the Fal. These have been polluted in consequence and the St Austell Bay area from the Gribben to Mevagissey has been seriously affected by these micaceous deposits. The extent of this must be seen to be appreciated.

The River Boards have, in recent years, been moving towards a prohibition of the pollution and the result has been an attempt by the China Clay Association to find an alternative means of disposal of the effluent.

Their report was published on Thursday October 16th, 1969 and it contains a brief summary of the problems, the scope, the possibilities and proposals. The possibilities for disposing of the mica are mainly two fold:

(a) Having mica lagoons on their own land or on land adjacent, which would in the case of the Goss Moor Scheme, contain the situation for at least 60 years or

(b) by pumping it through a pipe line of about 11 miles to an outfall approximately 880 yards South West of Menease Point near Gorran Haven, an area of outstanding natural beauty near the famous Dodman Point, all which is National Trust land. The plan is known as the Menease Point Scheme and would cost less than the Goss Moor Scheme.

Feared implications of the implementation of the China Clay Association's plans insofar as the Parish of Gorran is concerned.

1. Many stages in the construction of the pipeline would have a serious effect on the whole village of Gorran Haven and especially on:

   (a) the area of Lamledra and
   (b) the approach roads to it.

The period of construction could not be a short one because the tunnel from the vicinity of Lamledra to the proposed outfall would involve the removal of approximately 8,000 cubic yards of rock and subsoil. Any extension of the tunnel would add approximately 5,000 cubic yards per half mile. The removal of the said 8,000 cubic yards would in terms of lorry loads be about 1,600. In addition aggregate and cement or ready mixed concrete would be coming to the pithead and these would not, in every case, be the lorries engaged in removing the debris. Furthermore, heavy equipment would be required at Lamledra together with all pithead equipment. In all probability overhead cables would be necessary to bring the power to the site.

The present access roads from the Triangle to Lamledra are winding and narrow. Indeed, from Wayside onwards the movement of heavy lorries would preclude pedestrians and normal traffic unless the road were widened. A two-way traffic system is an alternative but Foxhole Lane is not practicable for lorries and the road across the Grooda would in turn, lead to a winding lane to the main Gorran Haven - St Austell Road, and use of this must be considered unthinkable.

If the project were carried out during a period involving the Summer, the whole of the area mentioned would be denied to the tourists, and the noise of lorries, possibly working round the clock would most surely be anything but conducive to a quiet seaside holiday. A winter operation would beggar description.

The main operational headquarters at Lamledra would of necessity be vast with dumping ground, turning areas etc.

It is abundantly clear therefore, that this outstanding area of natural beauty would be scarred permanently because the removal of the trees would be a necessity and no amount of post operative landscaping would recover the natural beauty nor the Cornish lanes and hedgerows.

2. According to a deposition signed by the fishermen of Gorran Haven, who are not only men of great experience but also have had handed down to them the knowledge of their forefathers from time immemorial, having given careful thought and consideration to the plan set out by the China Clay Association, they believe that if the effluent (1 1/2 million tons per year or 4,000 tons per day doubling in twenty years) of micaceous residue is pumped into the sea at the position shown on the map, the following result:-

   (a) The area affected by the micaceous residue would be much greater than that shown on the map.

(b) The area to landward of the outfall would be affected considerably and the residue would be deposited on the beaches and rocks adjacent to the outfall. Vault Beach and the area around Gorran Haven would receive some of the residue and the effects would be cumulative. The whole area from Point Head to Gerrans Bay would be affected in varying degrees. At certain periods according to wind and tide, the effects of the so called plume would be considerable. Fishing would be seriously affected in the neighbourhood of the outfall and the Trawl ground, plus the famous Dodman Fishing grounds, would be adversely affected.

Clearly, even if the fishermen are right in part only, the result would be disastrous. Gorran Haven's residents are mainly retired people and those who gain their livelihood from the Tourist Industry. The former would lose the amenities of this picturesque area and the latter would lose much trade. Indeed, Gorran Haven attracts mainly families with young children who can play on the clean sand or in the clear water and these families would no longer wish to come to Gorran Haven. Furthermore, during the construction of the pipeline etc. visitors would either be driven away or would not come. Compensation could not easily cover this because clientele is built up over a period of years and once the holiday cycle is broken the effect is felt for some years, and will have undeniable short and long term effects on property values.

Conclusion

The inhabitants of the Parish of Gorran are neither unaware of, nor unsympathetic to the difficulties faced by the China Clay Association over the disposal of micaceous residue, nor are they unaware of the value of the industry to their neighbours in the St. Austell area and to the Country generally. Moreover, they are pleased that the Association is endeavouring to cease pollution of the rivers in their area and the coastline around St Austell Bay.

Nevertheless they stoutly resist the inference that one of the most beautiful stretches of coastline in the British Isles should be sacrificed on the altar of industrial requirements and respectfully suggest that the China Clay Association disposes of its own residue within its own territory as outlined in its proposals. This project prejudices neither natural beauty, good agricultural land, the rights of the general public nor the livelihood of anyone in the China Clay Industry. In fact the additional cost to the Association would serve the locality by providing additional employment.

Since the publication of the China Clay Association's plans in October 1969, opposition to the pipe-line scheme has increased, not only locally but nationally. Fears have grown that the implemented scheme will pollute a much more extensive length of coastline than was originally envisaged. For this reason, many communities and local authorities well to the south-west of Gorran Haven have expressed grave anxiety about the possibility of wide-spread pollution. The Town Council of Penryn, for example, more than 15 miles down the coast, decided in March, 1970, to oppose the C.C.A. proposal.

It became obvious to the Residents' Association at an early date that only a full public inquiry can finally avert this threat to the South Cornish sea and beaches. The costs of such an inquiry are sure to be very high, and, while the clay industry can easily afford to pay its share, the Gorran and District Residents' Association felt that the small community it represents would be desperately hard-pressed to raise enough money to meet the charges of the legal and other experts necessary to present and win the conservationist case.

To raise cash for this purpose, the Residents' Association have accordingly set up the Gorran and District Coast anti-pollution Fund under the distinguished patronage of Sir John Betjeman (President of the Association), Commander Peter Scott, John Pardoe, M.P., Michael Foot, M.P., and Tony Soper. Any contributions to the Fund should be made payable to Gorran anti-pollution Fund and addressed to G.R. Ablett, Esq., Rice Farm, Gorran Haven, St. Austell, Cornwall. They will be most gratefully acknowledged and will be devoted solely to the campaign against china-clay pollution.

Already the pipe-line issue has aroused much interest in national newspapers and periodicals as well as on T.V. In January 1970, The New Statesman devoted a three-page feature article by its editor, Paul Johnson, which condemned the C.C.A.'s proposal as 'threatened assassination' of the South Cornish coast. And Commander Peter Scott has gone on record that 'the people will demand that pollution be controlled, and will not be fobbed off with short-term economic arguments. I believe the ultimate consensus will be that "the mess must be cleared up by those who made it"…. I think it very unlikely in the present climate of opinion that the pipe-line proposal will be allowed to go through: and that climate seems to me likely to harden against even "some dis-colouration of the sea" off the Dodman.'

In conclusion, it should be noted that the Gorran and District Residents' Association have already instructed an eminent firm of Consulting Engineers who, after a preliminary investigation, have advised that back-filling the clay-waste within the china-clay workings (representing a third alternative to (a) and (b) overleaf) is a viable possibility. In consequence of this advice, the C.C.A. has already instructed its own Consulting Engineers to consider this method of disposal.

(c)   The Result

The China Clay companies had promised that if there was proof that the micaceous residue would come ashore, they would not proceed with their scheme.

In the face of increasing doubt and opposition, they chartered a coaster to pump 300 tons of the residue into the sea just East of the Dodman. This contained radio-active isotopes which were plotted by another chartered vessel over six months. The fishermen's fears were proved correct, and the scheme was shelved.

Such was the relief that the Vicar, Canon Sturdy, conducted a service of thanksgiving in St. Goran Parish Church, attracting a large congregation.

Here I must pay tribute to the China Clay companies and especially to all the senior management who conducted negotiations with the Residents' Association's Committee of which I was Chairman. Not only were they true to their word, but also they showed no ill-feeling, no resentment and impeccable friendliness at all times.

There is no doubt that the Companies' proposals, had they been implemented, would have solved their greatest problem which still faces them today. I am equally sure if implemented, Gorran Haven and its environs would never be the same again.

This purely factual synopsis of the 'China Clay Fight' makes no mention of the emotional upheaval which the China Clay Association's proposals caused in the parish.

The formation of the Residents' Association to co-ordinate opposition to the scheme was bitterly opposed by some parishioners, albeit a small minority, and feelings ran high. However, the Residents' Association Committee, elected almost willy-nilly from the floor at a special meeting of objectors to the scheme, were later found to include a scientist, an engineer, an agriculturalist, a writer, a publicity officer and a journalist, while the secretary had been the personal assistant to a city solicitor; it was a formidable and talented team. To crown our good fortune, at the very outset an eminent Q.C. mapped out our campaign for us in three sentences:-

a) Engage consultants of equal status to those of the C.C.A.

b) Instruct them to find an acceptable and feasible alternative method of disposing of the micaceous residue.

c) Raise a five figure sum to enable this to be done.

The Committee undaunted, did not demur; the fight was on.

A fund raising committee was formed and these wonderful people - mainly of the fair sex - worked tirelessly and relentlessly for the next two years to ensure the money was available. It was a superb example of community spirit which engendered a camaraderie and selflessness akin to that of the war years. Everyone gave freely of time and substance neither asking for nor receiving thanks: the objective was paramount and it was achieved.

'A great multitude of fishes' (Luke 56)

FISH IN PLENTY

Former Plymouth librarian Bill Best-Harris, a devoted Westcountryman, said that the first records of a fishery in Gorran Haven date back to 1272, over seven centuries ago. It continued, and indeed thrived, until the 1960s and today only Lewis Billing, now in his eighties, is the only survivor of that long line of rugged men who from boyhood to old age, made their living from the sea around our shore.

But few realise the sheer size of our fishery in the 19th Century due to a booming Pilchard industry when these little fish were often too numerous to cope with. They were trapped in huge seines shot under the direction of huers on the cliff. These seines were about 300 yards long and 15 yards deep in the middle, the ends being narrower. The boats needed to carry the nets and the fish were of necessity large, stable and beamy.

Some idea of the size of the catches may be gained from the haul taken by the 'Zealous' seine (each had its own name) on 25th September, 1869 at Hemmick Beach. It totalled 400 hogsheads (barrels or casks) equivalent to about a million pilchards. Some catch! It was hard work but also dangerous with so much at stake, and in 1804, four men were drowned and two thrown on the rocks at the Deadman when trying to save the seine and the catch, in worsening weather.

Another fine haul was in October, 1874, when a Gorran seine caught nearly a ton and a half of very large mullet. The Brunel bridge at Saltash had already been built so the fish were landed at Mevagissey and sent to London.

The famous 'Zealous' seine was put up for auction at the Barley Sheaf on 21st March, 1879, together with boats and cellar materials. Particulars, the advertisement said, could be obtained from my great-grandfather, John Teague, a seiner who probably had a sixteenth share. No record of the sum raised is available but the sale caused a stir.

Perhaps the most interesting sale of the century took place in February, 1815. It was that of the 'Union Cellar', described as 'conveniently situated near the beach at Gorran Haven, containing five seine lofts with salt houses and capable of curing 800 hogsheads annually'.

This, in weight of cured fish, was 3,200 cwts. Just imagine the hive of activity that there was on the beach - and there was no quay between 1840 and 1886.

It is truly remarkable that this cellar, known for many years as the Big Cellar, remains virtually as it was 150 years ago, lofts and all. Its construction is remarkable, its ground floor a revelation.

'Driving boats' (for drift netting) up the slipway from the beach, the Watch-house, the Lime Kiln, the old Ship Inn and Fort - all the heart of the old fishery and associated activity - have also changed but little over those years.

With Pin-tables, Juke boxes and ugly conversions fronting so many little seaside communities like ours, are we not fortunate to have that almost unchanged piece of history down by our beach? And let's keep it that way.

'You can't choose your ancestors: that's fair they probably wouldn't have chosen you.' (Adam Smith)

THE SMITH CONNECTION WITH GORRAN

'Dalby Smith, St. Blazey' is the caption on most of the photographs of life in Mid-Cornwall during the 50 odd years between about 1875 and 1930. He was, in fact, born and bred in Gorran, only moving to St. Blazey after his photographic business was well established. Indeed 'Dalby Smith, Gorran' appears on all his early photographs.

Dalby was the youngest son of William Potter and Avis Maria Smith of Gorran Churchtown. William came from a Polruan sea-faring family which owned small ketches which plied the South Coast. A poor sailor, William became a mason and came to Gorran in 1833 to build the Gorran Church rooms. While the work was continuing, he met and fell in love with Avis Maria Michell of Boswinger but the match was frowned upon by the Michell family of yeomen farmers. Undaunted, they eloped and were married on 22nd March, 1843 by Rev. Thomas Trevenen, Rector of St. Ewe.

Their eldest son, William, became the local carpenter and undertaker at Gorran, his workshop being where the garage of the house at the corner of the Cotna turning stands.

Their second son, Guy, had a wagonette plying from Gorran to St. Austell and in 1878 he brought to Gorran a Miss Tryphena Hodge from Plymouth, to become the first school-mistress to teach at the new Board School with Mr. Joseph Treneer. Guy said he would marry her or no-one else: he married her in 1882. She died in 1891 and he never married again. Guy was also the 'dentist' for Gorran and Mevagissey and he had a full set of instruments. Some old inhabitants of the area still recall his 'cold steel' extractions.

Dalby Smith was named after the Rev. Dalby, one-time vicar of Gorran, whose sister married a Michell of Boswinger. The name is still carried on to this day through Dalby Michell who continues to farm at Boswinger. Curiously, Miss Hodge was the daughter of a Plymouth photographer who was a contemporary of Dalby Smith, but it is not known if the photographic connection was coincidental or not.

Dalby Smith had one son who was not interested in photography and moved to London. It is believed that all his father's plates were destroyed.

Guy Smith's son, Archie, joined the Royal Navy in 1907 and served in both World Wars. As a Petty Officer, he spent five years in the battle-cruiser Inflexible and was present at the battles of the Falkland Islands, Jutland and the Dardanelles.

His daughter, Ruth Avis was for many years an infant teacher at Gorran School and now lives in Torquay, and I am his son.

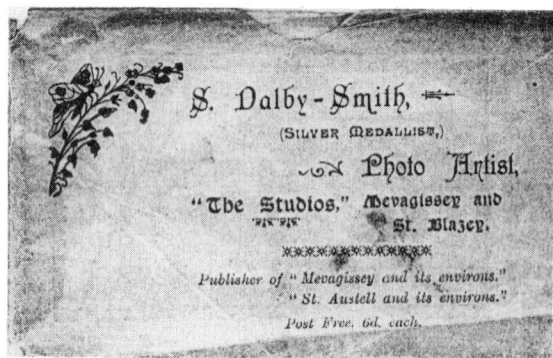

S. Dalby Smith, my great uncle and a celebrated mid-Cornwall photographer. Note the hyphen between Dalby and Smith. Tut! Tut! It should be plain Smith! We think the model is his mother Avice Maria because of her firm Michell features.

'Try to understand silence: it's worth listening to' (Harry Truman)

LISTENING FOR 'TICKERS'

As a boy living in Gorran Haven between the wars, I spent every spare moment of my life either among the fishermen on the beach or the 'old men' who sat on a long seat in front of the Lime-Kiln wall and reminisced. Even as late as the early 1930s there was no mains water, no electricity, no drainage; it was almost medieval.

We children made our own fun but most of it in so far as the boys were concerned, was associated with the beach, the harbour, the sea, cliffs and rocks. When the crabbers landed their catches we helped to bring the 'mawns' up to the Co-op (where the Mermaid Café now stands) to be packed in barrels and sent live by the two o'clock train from St. Austell to Billingsgate. Quite often there would be about eight or even more barrelfuls and as you entered the store you could hear them - ticking, something akin to the ticking of some clocks, but unmistakable.

From an early age I learnt to put this knowledge of a crab's 'ticking' to good use by listening for it among the clefts in the rocks at dead low water during Spring tides. If a crab is there you'll hear it. My best catch was about 1954 when on a glorious August day with the sea like a millpond, my wife and I went down to Penveor Cove, east of the Dodman, to listen out. There wasn't a ripple as I jumped ashore and made for a cleft I knew and not a sound came from anywhere. Suddenly, I heard it - loud and clear - and as I squeezed into the cleft I could see a large crab which had jammed itself in. I tip-toed away and called for the gaff. With great care lest I caused it to flex its big claws and be unmoveable, I yanked it out at a stroke. It was a seven pound cock crab in prime condition.

When we returned to the beach to 'moor up', Jack Patten, a hardbitten fisherman with a soft heart which he tried to hide, spotted the crab and said "Where did 'ee git 'ee boy?" "Ashore down Penveor," I replied. "Ah," said Jack with a broad smile, "you 'eard'n ticking." He knew in a second.

Maybe there are no seven pound cock-crabs around today, but who knows? It's a thrill to catch a ticker, whatever the size, so try it this Summer.

Seek and ye shall find (Matthew 77)

THE QUEST FOR FRUITS DE MER ON THE SEASHORE

Isaac Walton wrote that God never did make a more calm, quiet, innocent recreation than fishing, and how right he was: it is so rewarding in every way. The fisherman does not always need a boat, a rod, a net, even a line; there are simple fishing pursuits such as hunting for Razor-Shells, a delicacy to some.

In pre-war days this was quite a common practice on Gorran Haven beach at low water, Spring tide, about April. The area where these Skipper-long-boys, as we called them, were found was between Quay Head and Red Rock. The sea had to be calm and some sun was always helpful, and in these conditions the hunt was on. But we did not use salt, being much more deft than the westerners! We looked for the tell-tale little hole in the smooth sand and we knew the fish was just below. Very stealthily, we approached this mark, bent down beside it and with a quick thrust of the hand into the sand about three inches below the mark, the razor-shell was contacted and held by a sideways pressure. (This prevented it from making its escape downwards which it could do at remarkable speed).

The other hand was then pushed underneath the skipper-long-boy and gently lifted - not pulled - out or you end up with just the shells. One could catch about a dozen of these in half an hour but usually blood flowed quite freely from the hand used to trap them. They are not called Razor-shells without reason! I did not fancy the tough-looking flesh and never ate them but most locals roasted them on the bars of their Cornish range and ate them with gusto.

'Evil is wrought by want of thought.' (Thomas Hood)

THOUGHTLESSNESS - A SOBERING RESULT

When I was at Gorran School from 1927 until 1934, the boys were for ever playing with something - a ball if we had one, hoops, air guns, bows and arrows, carbide to make explosives, sticks, stones, indeed anything we could lay our hands on.

Peashooters were popular at times, especially when 'aglets' (haws) or ivy berries were available, and so were water pistols and yo-yos if we could afford one.

About 1933 potato pistols were the rage. The gun had a spring which was pushed back to recoil when the nozzle was pushed into a potato. This nozzle had a little barrel where the piece of potato lodged and all was then cocked ready for action. The velocity was not great but it was good fun, and we all had one each so we would 'pick up sides' and fight like cowboys.

One day, I went to school, gun in one pocket and the other stuffed with potatoes: I liked plenty of ammunition. But to my horror, soon after the battle commenced after school, my pistol refused to operate so I threw it away and set off home on my own, across the footpath past the garage to the top of Gorran Haven hill.

As I walked along dejectedly I became aware of this useless ammunition so I took a large potato out of my pocket and flung it away, full force. Will Richards' cows were grazing nearby and to my horror, the potato hit a cow on the forehead as it looked at me. But worse was to come; it slowly sank to its knees and on to the ground. The enormity of the deed struck home - I had killed one of Will Richards' cows. Horror struck, I set off home as fast as I could go. Coleridge describes the situation precisely:-

'Like one, that on a lonesome road
Doth walk in fear and dread,
And having once turned round, walks on
And turns no more his head.'

When I got home at Elmsdale I tried to act normally but my mother intuitively saw that everything was not normal. She looked me straight in the face and said, "You've been up to something; what have you done?" In a contrite voice I replied, "I've killed one of Will Richards' cows."

"What?" she almost screamed, "you've killed one of Will Richards' cows? What are you talking about?"

Confession may be good for the soul but it is hard going. In simple terms I had nearly told the full story, when she interrupted angrily and said, "We'll be ruined; that cow is worth £20," and followed up with her being unable to pay the rates and everything else.

"I wish I could die," I said to myself, utterly helpless, but guilty of it all.

"Go on up to Willie Richards and tell him what you've done," she ordered and anxious though I was at the thought, it was a relief to get away from my mother's withering onslaught.

I was never a long-distance runner, but I ran past Rice and up the hill, overtook Harry Morse's pony cart and jumped over the stile near the seat, over the next stile to the murder field. Still breathless, I looked anxiously for the dead cow - and there she was, on her feet and grazing peacefully.

We had heard all about the Relief of Lucknow and the Relief of Mafeking but my relief was infinitely greater, I can assure you.

Oh dear! I forgot that Samuel Johnson said that a man should be careful never to tell tales of himself to his disadvantage.

.... they will be remembered and brought against him upon some subsequent occasion.

Man is the hunter; woman is his game (Tennyson)

BODRUGAN BROAD LANE

Up to 1914, there was an area between Mevagissey and Gorran which had a special significance to young men and women from both communities. It was (and still is to some) known as Bodrugan Broad Lane - an ill-defined section of road, but could include any part between the top of Bodrugan Hill and the Barley Sheaf sign where the two Gorran roads meet. It was always a desolate part of the road between Mevagissey and Gorran as those who have 'walked it' on a dark winter's night will know, but at the turn of the century it was almost 'Lovers' Lane' on Sunday nights. At that time, chapels in both villages were full for the evening service: it was de rigueur to 'go chapel'.

To illustrate this, I recall taking an evening service at Fore Street Methodist Chapel in Mevagissey (now demolished in favour of council houses). This chapel held about six hundred - it was that big!. When I went into the vestry that evening in the early 1950s, the steward Mr. Jack Prynn said to me, "I don't know how many we'll have tonight my boy. When I was a young man if you weren't in a seat by half past five, you had to sit in the stairs." And so it was at the 'Bryanites' Chapel (River Street) now closed, and the Congregational Chapel too. The four chapels in Gorran parish were the same.

So when the services ended the eligible chaps and maids made for Bodrugan Broad Lane where many romances began. But Mevagissey men had to be careful; if they married a Gurran maid, to Gurran they had to go.

So when you walk that lonely road again and hear a shriek or two, do not be frightened; they are only echoes of a romantic past.

'A game conceived in heaven' (Neville Cardus)

GORRAN AND CRICKET

Village cricket is synonymous with rural England and a warm, sunny Summer Saturday afternoon and Cornwall epitomised it perfectly. There were two small villages in Cornwall where cricket was more than a Saturday afternoon's recreation for its young men and a quiet, relaxing change from the daily grind for the older ones - it almost challenged religion. Those villages were Gorran and Troon, near Camborne, both of which reached the very top by being champions of Cornwall and winning the Western Morning News Challenge Cup.

I was not born into a cricketing - or indeed, a sporting - family. My paternal grandfather, Guy Smith, was a true gun and dog countryman but he was living with his daughter, a Coastguard's wife at Padstow, and my scene was the beach, the school and the Chapel.

But there was no escape from cricket. All boys in the parish played it, talked it, lived it and it was serious business. Even as we walked to school we picked up stones and bowled them at something, while the shortest of short seasons for our kick-and-rush football in hobnail boots never took the place of bat and ball.

The old cricket field, next to the School and now the School field, was hallowed turf and all those who played on it were heroes. Even the two greatest stonewallers of all time who played for the second team were in that category. Frank Ivey could never be tempted to put bat to ball till all the fielders crowded in on him and then he lashed out, scattering all of them to the four corners of the field. Francis Guy could not be tempted to make a run. How many heroes of the game could beat Francis who on one occasion opened the innings for that illustrious 2nd XI and having lost all ten others, remained 0 not out at the end?

Then there were Maurice Hurrell, Tommy Guy, Ern Liddicoat, Les Rowse, Herbert and Harold Bunney, Jack Hurrell, Bill May, Warrick and Reg Kendall, Howard and Stan Whetter, who were the first team.

The Saturday 1st team home games were Eastern League matches, life and death affairs. The old wooden pavilion which served as a tea-room (there were no players' changing rooms) was furnished with wooden trestles and forms, and the Ladies' Tea Committee of players' wives, provided teas which were second to none. Yes, only the best at Gorran. The smell of saffron cake, yeast cake, fruit cake, splits and a generous topping of cream, freshly cut bread and butter, plus the hot, steaming tea permeated the wooden shed: it was all magic.

On the field Maurice Hurrell broke visitors' stumps for a pastime with his fast off-the-pitch balls like those of Maurice Tate of Sussex and England. Tommy Guy, easy action, quick and accurate bowled at the other end while Howard Whetter with a wrist action and accurate off breaks was a fine first change. And all the time Ern Liddicoat at square point stood poised like a predator ready to strike. All we boys knew that our opponents were out to beat Gorran, yea, at all costs. We knew that our batsmen never got their legs in front of the wicket and would never be caught behind: indeed, we knew that Gorran would never be beaten fairly! And this was proved beyond doubt when Gorran won the Championship in 1937.

And then the war came. Sometime in the next six years that green wooden pavilion blew away in a gale and the few who remained salvaged what they could and hid it: the field looked forlorn indeed.

I played for the St. Austell County School side before the war, but was never considered for the Gorran 1st team even though in 1939 I played for Cornwall Under 19 (the Colts) and with some distinction. But that is not a criticism of the Gorran selectors, because it never occurred to me at any time that I was good enough to replace any of that team: I knew I was not, and that is surely an indication of the standard played at Gorran at that time.

In 1942 I was called up for aircrew training in the R.A.F., and I was ordered to report to the mecca of all cricketers the world over - yes, Lord's Cricket Ground. So with a badly poisoned fore-finger resulting from a stab from the spine of a stinking Wrasse when crabbing, I turned up at those pearly gates. Our billets were at Regent's Park but Lord's was where we did our initial work. As I looked out over that hallowed ground, I visualised Larwood, Voce, Hobbs, Hutton, Aussies and all, with the eager crowd all round, but what was before my eyes? The square had been cordoned off, but everywhere else sheep were grazing in a most peaceful, country scene. Oh, what an anti-climax; there was a war on, and we disciples of the noble game of cricket, were in it.

I did not touch a bat or ball until I was demobilised, by which time cricket had gone from my mind entirely. I followed the Victory tests from afar but took an interest in the Australian, Christofani, whom I knew in the R.A.F.

But the spirit of cricket had not died in Gorran and as far as I am aware, the man who rekindled the flame in the Parish was Ern Liddicoat. One day, I was working in my allotment at Parc an Gates when Ern approached me.

"I'm trying to start up the cricket team again, Archie; what about it?"

"No, Ern," I replied, "I haven't played for years, I've got no gear, I've got my boat down and I don't think I'll start again."

"Aw," said he, "don't be like that: think about it," and off he went.

I didn't think about it but Ern did and some days later turned up again and said, "We're playing Philleigh at Philleigh on Saturday and Featherstone will lend you a pair of trousers. I'll take 'ee down."

I went. I have entirely forgotten everything about that game except one thing. Having no boots, I wore white pumps which I had as a P.E. teacher. The field was cleared of cows before we started but their trademarks remained and alas, I slipped on one, went down flat and came home with Featherstone's trousers hall marked.

From that day on, I played for Gorran until 1958 and during those years we won the Cornwall County Championships twice. All of it is history for someone to write sometime, but my greatest disappointment has been the lack of cricketing zeal amongst our youngsters in the Parish, so unlike that of the boys and men of my youth.

I attended two M.C.C. coaching courses in the 1950s, one when the M.C.C. coaching manual was thrashed out and later, when the M.C.C. Advanced course was instituted to train Coaches to run courses and award Coaching Certificates to successful candidates. I organised and ran several in the County, mainly for teachers, but also for club players if there was room. These courses taught every technique of bowling, batting and fielding of this most un-natural of all games. It was an opportunity my pals and I would have given our right arms for.

One day at Gorran in 1956, a very promising young batsman came into the pavilion, having been caught at extra cover, and said as he threw down his bat, "That's the third time I've been caught at extra cover."

I told him that the reason was simple: he was leading with his left foot down the wicket and was not getting it to the ball. "Lead with your head," I told him, "then your foot will follow to the pitch of the ball. Eh, come up to the nets of Wednesday night and I'll bowl you a few overs so you can practise it!"

"No," replied he, "I'll have another knock next Saturday."

That was a bitter disappointment to me, and in hindsight, I believe it was the beginning of a general lack of sheer enthusiasm and keenness among youngsters which is essential if standards are to improve. Those qualities, worthy though they are, are not enough in themselves - there must be an opportunity for those virtues to be developed. This is where coaching comes in and the reason is clear. Cricket is an un-natural game. There are only two strokes in the whole of batting which are natural movements; the rest are not, and have to be learnt. The correct techniques have to be taught and learnt. They have to be practised and practised until the wrong techniques are eradicated and the correct ones become a reflex action. That calls for dedication, determination and stamina. But it is worthwhile; batsmen can be made even if bowlers are born.

When one reflects on the game, it will be seen that in fact, cricket is a sideways game: you stand sideways-on to bat, you bowl sideways-on and you field and throw in the same way.

To be perhaps fair to present day youth, there are so many distractions in so many directions, and so much opportunity to pursue them, that there are too many pulls away from the sideways game. But the price to be paid for excellence remains the same as it ever was, and there is no short cut.

In 1953, Gorran won the County Championship at Penzance by defeating Falmouth by two wickets. All Gorran players were born within the sound of Gorran Church bells: that is a feat to be proud of.

'Genealogy: tracing yourself back to people better than you are.'
(John Pollard)

THE BILLING FAMILY

If you look at the name Billing listed in the Cornwall and Isles of Scilly telephone directory, you will see that there are about 50 in number.

Many of these Billings originated from Gorran Haven where Billings were first mentioned in the 18th Century records. In the 1881 census, no less than 35 were named and there were scions in Canada and the U.S.A. as well, at that time.

The origin of the Billing family used to baffle its members and I clearly recall Mr. Britton, the master at Gorran School in the 1920s, stating that Billingsgate, the London fish market, was undoubtedly named after a Billing - much to the embarrassment of my friend Arthur.

So what do we know about them? Firstly, they are of Norman descent. After the Conquest, they were given lands in North Cornwall and for several hundred years they were people of some importance. Following their research of the Billing family of Hengar and Lank, Rebecca Chadburn and Irene Donald recorded that some became Burgesses and Knights of the Shires, and one was a helper to the Sheriff to collect money when the Black Prince was made a Knight.

In the 15th Century, astute marriages brought wealth and power to the family, and early in the 16th Century Hengar came into Billing hands. In 1620, Richard Billing, the heir, entered his pedigree and coat of arms (three stags' heads) on the visitation of the herald to Bodmin.

One of his daughters, Loveday, married William Hamley of Tregongeeves near St. Austell. After her husband's death, she became a Quaker and visited George Fox, the founder of the Society of Friends, when he was imprisoned in Launceston Gaol in 1656. She steadfastly refused to pay tithes and was also imprisoned in Launceston Gaol, but her spirit was never broken. She died in 1682 and was buried in the little Friends' burial ground at Tregongeeves which I clearly remember, before the road was widened opposite St. Mewan school and the graves removed.

A marriage also linked the Billings with the Bligh family of St. Tudy, of which Captain William Bligh of 'Bounty' fame was a member. Yet another Billing, according, to Dr. A.L. Rowse in his book 'Cornish in America,' might well have replaced William Penn in American history.

Clearly, Billing is a name imprinted on history books for posterity, but what about those Gorran Haven Billings? Could they be descendants of that famous Hengar family?

The family tree of the Hengar Billings shows that in 1667, a John Billing married a Jane Cock and their great-grandson, also a John, a seaman, married an Elizabeth Broad in the year 1747. They had a large family of six sons and five daughters whose descendants, as far as I am aware, have not been traced.

Perhaps coincidentally, the Broad family owned considerable property in Gorran parish and their names are recorded in our Church records from the early 17th Century onwards.

Similarly, the Cocks were an old Gorran family, also dating from the early 17th Century. So the Billings, Cocks and Broads were related by marriage, but did a Hengar Billing, perhaps a sea-farer, come to Gorran Haven?

A possible clue involves one James Billing who made a will dated May 6th, 1807. He lived in Gorran Haven and described himself as 'poorly in body but of sound mind' but he was no poor fisherman. James bequeathed a house and £50 to one son; a house and £40 to another; the cellar under the two dwellings and £50 to a third son; £60 to his daughter, Elizabeth; £25 to his grand-daughter, Grace Cock, and to his son-in-law, one sixteenth part of the pilchard seine called the New Seine. He also bequeathed one shilling to Grace Broad Billing who was my great-great-grandmother. The residue went to his wife Elizabeth.

This estate was a fortune. The will still in the possession of Jessica Johns, née Billing, who is a direct descendant of old James. Her father, Eddie could never understand how his grandfather was a comparatively wealthy man at a time when it was as much as fishermen could do to keep the wolf from the door? Did it come from the Hengar connection?

Even the epitaph on a tomb of the Hengar Billings seems to fit the rather serious, sober Billings of Gorran Haven. It reads:-

As you pass by, cast an eye;
As you are now, so once was I;
As I am now so you must be.
Prepare for Death, and follow me.

Addendum

Since completing the above, a distant relative, Donovan Michell, who is a keen genealogist, has given me more information. A Joseph Broad married Grace Melhuish both of Gorran in 1781 and their daughter, Grace married James Billing (Junr.) in 1805. Their daughter Fanny Broad Billing married Gabriel Shear in 1832 and they were my great-great-grandparents. The blood line of the Broads has been traced back to the Plantagenets, and William of Normandy.

You will clearly see that the purpose of genealogy is to trace yourself back to people better than you are: I make no further comment because of my modest nature!

'I must go down to the seas again, to the lonely sea and the sky.' (John Masefield)

HEAVEN ON EARTH BY THE SEA

'Laughs and Sweet Memories,' which I wrote in 1992 to recall my boyhood between the wars in Gorran Haven, caused many people whose minds had been stirred by it, to write to me with little reminiscences of their own, knowing that I would treasure them. Here is one written by Winifred Warren (née Billing) who is now 87 years of age and is living near Alton, Hants.

I was born in 1911 and my father Peter Billing, brother of Bert, was a cousin of Wallace and Cyrus Coombe, Leonard Billing and Isabel's mother, Emily.
My father really never left Gorran Haven and his heart was always there, so my sister Leonie and I never became Devonians and were always 'Gorran maids'.
My father's holiday - few had one - always started on the Thursday before August bank holiday (which was the first Monday in August) so this allowed him to extend his holiday over two week-ends, but our holiday was indefinite and was never less than a month. Previous to that Thursday arrangements had to be made regarding transport from St. Austell station to Gorran Haven. If it was just our family of four we hired the pony trap of Will Cloke in Mevagissey. If we were meeting others, we had Nick Liddicoat's wagonette. On arrival at St. Austell there was great excitement. We liked the wagonette - it was fun - especially if Wallace Coombe was in the party. Nick had a pretty dry sense of humour and with Wallace there too, there was a ride of a life-time to come and laughs galore.
We always left St. Austell by the higher road to Pentewan past the Trenarren turn, stopping at the top of the hill into Pentewan to put the 'drags' or 'shoes' on the back wheels to steady the vehicle down the hill. It was always a friendly, unhurried journey with people waving or calling a greeting as we passed. We continued past Pentewan beach. The coastal road had not been built so we went up the old steep hill to the Gorran-Mevagissey road. If it was the wagonette we turned right and through High Lanes to

Gorran. The trap however, turned left at the junction and went down the hill, past the school into the Square and up Polkirt Hill. At Portmellon we went across the sand at the top of the beach and up Bodrugan Hill. Only children rode up the hill - adults walked. Once we got up to the top before our parents and Mr. Cloke said, "Shall we go on without them?" We were terrified and I never passed that spot again without remembering that moment of panic. Then came the long 'Bodrugan Broad Lane' as it was known, down Sheep's Lane and home: heaven on earth by the sea. Out we got to the welcome of familiar, friendly faces and smiles everywhere; we had arrived.

P.S. Wallace Coombe became a guard on the G.W.R. and during the war was frequently on the Penzance-Plymouth or London run. At St. Austell station he was ever on the look-out for Gorran people and many a time I rode from St. Austell to Plymouth in his guard's van talking about home. We resented stops en route which interrupted our talk!

Like many others, he had left Gorran Haven but his heart remained there for ever.

*'For oft when on my couch I lie
In vacant or in pensive mood,
They flash upon that inward eye'
(Wordsworth)*

No, not daffodils but memories, memories which have sunk so deeply that they were almost forgotten. And then, someone - or even someone's name - brings back that which was almost forgotten with a remarkable freshness.

And so it was with me when my old friend Winifred (see Heaven on earth by the sea) wrote to me and included the following:-

'My eyesight has failed, so writing is a problem, but my memory is the sharper! I enjoy remembering the sounds of early Summer mornings when the men were preparing to go to sea - the bellows, the thud of the heavy sea-boots, the cry of the gulls! I am so grateful to have had such experiences. Thank-you for renewing so much for me.'

That set off a chain reaction of memories in my mind, especially the two words 'bellows' and 'sea-boots'. Few today would appreciate the significance of them. Until the late 1920s little had changed in the way of life at Gorran Haven. There was no electricity, no mains water, no sewage disposal. Light came from candles or paraffin lamps, water from a village pump and sewage was 'disposed of'. Cooking and heating came from the old Cornish Range, Zeboed every afternoon until it shone. In the evening it was 'open fire' and in the morning 'turned in' to direct the heat towards the oven. But 'first thing' it had to be lit: it was rarely, if ever, kept in overnight for economic reasons and fire was always a great fear. In fact, as a small boy, I clearly remember the sound of my grandmother throwing water on the dying embers just before she came up to bed, as well as the peculiar smell of the steam which came up the stairs to permeate my bedroom.

But back to first thing! Kindling wood was usually in short supply, few had newspapers, paraffin was too dear, so it was hard going to get the fire lit and that is where the bellows (pronounced hereabouts 'billies') came in. A few sparks or a tiny flame were encouraged by that remarkable invention when used with skill - not too hard to blow out the bit of life but enough to keep the little flame going. Winifred had heard the huffing and puffing of the bellows as she lay in bed and it reminded her of lighting the fire 'first thing', boiling the 'kittle' and then down to breakfast. How little things of no real consequence can trigger off experiences of eighty years earlier!

The other words which she used 'the thud of heavy sea-boots' also took me back - and even further. There were no rubber boots in those days and the fishermen wore heavy-grade leather, hand made boots to the knees or even just above. They were indeed heavy with thick studded soles and were almost inflexible. Little wonder, therefore, that the thud of these sea-boots just before dawn echoed down the narrow street as the crabbers made for their boats.

Those sea-boots always had a special significance to me. My grandfather, whose cottage in the street we shared, was apprenticed to Joseph Dingle, a shoemaker in Gorran, in 1867 when aged eleven. His main occupation after serving his apprenticeship was making those sea-boots. He was a skilled man but would never press his clients for payment, a practice which did not pay. Rather than press his debtors, he gave up shoemaking and went crabbing with his father and brother John. However, he kept his last, or foot as he called it, together with his tools and did our shoe-repairs. But his skill with his knife always fascinated me: the word deft does not begin to describe it!

This skill was manifested to me in two ways. First of all, he could cut a wafer-thin piece of bread and butter perfectly and with an old kitchen knife half worn away. Few can do that today with a bread knife or anything else. And secondly, he could cut two 'snades' from a mackerel at precisely the right thickness and shape so that when they were pulled through the water on a handline from a slow-moving boat, they simulated an eel so perfectly that his dexterity as a 'pollacker' was matchless. Even when eighty years of age, half bent, hands half closed and stiff, he would say to me when I came in from my boat, a thirteen foot six dinghy, "Don't moor her up boy, leave the line aboard. I'll go down Cadythew when 'tis high water."

And off he would go, feathering the Seraph's scoops like an expert oarsman. As a young man he worked his crab pots off the Gribben, at times having to help his sails with nine feet paddles: now he could handle something lighter.

He would always come back with a string of pollacks. As Bob Ball once remarked, "Billy Teague will catch pollack when there's none there."

William Teague never had a penny in his pocket throughout his life except on Sundays when my grandmother gave him a threepenny bit for collection at Chapel.

He died as he lived - penniless - but that saintly old man's memory is worth more to me than if he had left me a millionaire for life.

William Cowper once wrote:-

'What peaceful hours I once enjoyed!
How sweet their memory still!
But they have left an aching void
This world can never fill.

But I could say the same of people as well as of peaceful hours - and William Teague would be among the foremost of them.

'Home is the sailor, home from the sea'. (Requiem, R.L. Stevenson)

THOMAS SANDERS AND THE SHIP INN

The house at the bottom of Church Street, Gorran Haven, and now part of the Mermaid Café complex, was formerly a pub, the Ship Inn. Only one sign of its old role remains and that is a ring on the wall of the house facing the street; it was for hitching up horses while the owner had a drink.

In the second half of the 19th Century the landlord was a Thomas Sanders. Thomas was a Navy pensioner, and he had a favourite daughter named Mary, who married a local man, Samuel Collins Kerkin, on March 3rd, 1863. They emigrated to New Zealand in 1872.

Thomas kept a diary and this came into the possession of 'Boy Jim' Liddicoat (known as 'Boy Jim' locally to distinguish him from Ern's father who was 'Man Jim'). Boy Jim's mother's maiden name was Louie Ball and her brother Fred married a sister of Thomas Sanders. This no doubt explains how Boy Jim had the diary as the Sanders family emigrated. Fred Ball's son Charlie, born in 1875, was called up for the army in 1915 and was killed in France in 1917.

As a young man, Charlie fell in love with Laura Liddicoat. They married, and in 1909 had a daughter whom they named Ena Maud. When the Great War began, Charlie was already 39, far too old for war service. But such was the terrible loss of life in Flanders and on the Somme in particular, that Charlie was called up in 1917 and posted to a Worcestershire Regiment. It too was sent to the Somme where Charlie was severely wounded, succumbing to these injuries some time later: he never returned to England and was buried in France, at Etaples.

'Much drinking: little thinking'. (Jonathan Swift)

THE WRECK OF THE 'SHIP'?

Mrs. Christine Hammond, a keen historian and able researcher, has provided an interesting vignette about the 'Ship Inn'.

The 'Ship' was formerly called the 'Queen's Head', the name having been changed to the 'Ship' in 1820. No reason was given, but 1820 was the year when George III died and the Prince Regent acceded to the throne as George IV. His long-separated wife Caroline returned from the Continent to claim her position of Queen, but George induced his Cabinet to begin divorce proceedings. The fuss which ensued is most interesting, but the whole affair resulted in many more splits than that of the Royal couple! It seems reasonable to suppose that the 'Queen's Head' was no longer an appropriate name for the pub: the 'Ship Inn' was much safer all round!

Thomas Sanders (or Saunders) retired in 1866 and a Mr. Parks took over as manager on January 16th of that year. In 1867, Sanders sold all rights to a Mr. Vercoe who still maintained Parks as manager. However, Mr. Vercoe soon sold the pub to Hicks, the St. Austell brewers, for £61 but Parks continued as Hicks' manager.

So far so good - all sounds fine - but trouble lay ahead. In 1868, the Court at St. Austell renewed all public house licences for the area except one, the 'Ship Inn', which was refused. The reason was given. The landlord was misbehaving and holding a 'rowdy house'. There was a fiddler there every Saturday night and there was dancing on the sandy floor. Worse still, the beach was used for cock-fighting, bets were taken and it usually ended in a brawl.

The premises were bought by Mr Walter Beer in the late 19th Century. When they were sold by his daughter, Miss Lilian Beer, she inserted a condition on the deeds that it shall never again be a pub.

The stories of the 'goings on' at the old 'Ship' are well known to the village's older residents. I had never heard of cock-fighting there, so I mentioned it to Mrs. Jessica Johns (née Billing). "Oh yes", she said, "I've heard all about it and my father once got an Indian Game rooster from your grandfather, Guy Smith, and that rooster was so fierce, father was afraid to go into the run so he killed it and we had it for dinner".

I have always known that my grandfather bred Indian Game and that they were the cock-fighters' choice, but there is nothing to associate him with the Ship Inn's loss of its licence!

'Bring with thee, jest and youthful jollity'. (Milton, L'allegro)

Gorran Haven was not the only centre of jollity. In her delightful little booklet 'A History of Gorran' written by Christine Hawkridge (now Mrs. North, Cornwall County Archivist) in 1960, she records competition bell-ringing between parishes and in one held at Gorran in 1837, prizes were seven good silk hats, a sovereign for the runners-up and ten shillings for the third prize. "Good entertainment for men and horse" could be obtained at the New Inn, kept by Gabriel Shear. He was my great-great grandfather and though he was given an illustrious Christian name, our family will admit that he was no archangel.

There is but one inn at Gorran now, the Barley Sheaf. In the 16th Century it boasted four taverns.

'They that go down to the sea in ships'. (Psalm 107v23)

A SOBERING REMINDER

Summer storms of an extremely violent nature do occur from time to time.

Here is the record of one such storm exactly as written by Edward Harvey (Eddie) Billing in 1902. Eddie was the father of Mrs. Henry Johns, our 'Jessica Rose', now in her eighties.

"To bear record of the event when we suffered such damage with our mullet nets at Hemmick. The gale sprung up on July 25th, 1902, on a Friday and continued until Saturday night, the 26th. It came first from the S.S.E. and worked South about to South West and continued increasing, it being one of the worst gales on record in Summer season. We suffered far worse West of Deadman than East. We went out on the following Monday morning to recover the wreck.

A public tea was held in the Congregational schoolroom the same day, it being the Anniversary of the Chapel's Sunday School".

An interesting little account, but if we reflect, we clearly see the disastrous effect on the village as a whole at that time. Except for some pots or nets kept in reserve or perhaps were ashore for mending, all the fishermen's gear would have been out - crab pots, trammels, mullet nets, mackerel nets - the lot - and such a gale would have caught everything from the Eastern land up to the Gribben, to the Western land west of the Deadman: there was no shelter for any gear with the shifting wind whipping up the sea everywhere.

Losses were great, earnings were severely restricted and the winter of 1902 was one of hardship to the villagers.

What effect would such a gale have on the village today? Would we fear the coming winter?

AN INTERESTING ENTRY

On March 24th, 1882, Thomas Sanders made the following entry in his diary:-

'The Duke of Heddenburrow was at Gorran Haven'.

This intrigued me; I wondered if it was correct. I guessed that if it was, there would be some record in the local papers of the following week of this member of the Royal Family's visit and sure enough, there was - in the West Briton, and it proved that old Thomas was correct.

The report is fascinating, and here it is.

"THE DUKE OF EDINBURGH IN THE WEST

Her Majesty's despatch vessel Lively, Commander le Strange, arrived off Penzance harbour about 2 o'clock on Wednesday afternoon, having on board their Royal Highnesses, the Duke and Duchess of Edinburgh. The Duke drove to the Battery where the Royal Naval Reserves were inspected after which his Royal Highness walked back to his carriage, drove to the harbour and returned to the Lively in the steam launch.
Their Royal Highnesses arrived at Falmouth the same evening and landed on Thursday morning. H.R.H. proceeded to the R.N.R. battery where the men were put through the review exercise, H.R.H. expressing himself well satisfied and ordered the men a holiday in token thereof.
Her Royal Highness afterwards proceeded to St. Mawes and subsequently took a drive in the country. Her Royal Highness on going to a farmhouse for some cream, observed some young pigs, took a fancy to one, purchased it, bringing it back to the yacht.
The yacht left for Fowey on Friday morning and H.R.H. inspected several coastguard stations on the Cornish coast. In the evening the Royal Party landed at Cremyll."

N.B. The Duke of Edinburgh was Arthur, second son of Queen Victoria. He was born in 1844 and died in 1900. He would have been 38 years of age when he visited the Coastguard Station at Gorran Haven. It was he who laid the foundation stone of the present Eddystone Lighthouse in August 1879, and he also opened it on May 18th, 1882, two months after visiting Gorran Haven.

It occurred to me a short time ago that the present Duke of Edinburgh, who has a lively sense of humour, might be interested in the visit of his Royal ancestors to this remote fishing village well over a century ago and that Thomas Sander's spelling and the story of the little pig might be of interest too. So I wrote to him with this information and enclosed three copies of St. Just Church's history with a humble request that he might see fit to autograph them on behalf of our Restoration Fund.

As I had feared, it was intercepted by the Duke's equerry who replied that His Royal Highness regrettably could not undertake to carry out such requests. My stamped addressed envelope was returned but not the three copies! And that hurt! But the Archbishop of Canterbury has autographed three and was delighted to do so.

'A little child shall lead them.....' (Isaiah 116)

AN EXAMPLE TO FOLLOW: A LESSON TO REMEMBER

Just before Christmas 1943, I arrived in Moncton, New Brunswick from the Western Prairies of Canada with fellow R.A.F. pilots to await a ship back to England. Moncton, like many places on Canada's Eastern seaboard, has many people of Scottish descent, and these good people were anxious to give hospitality to us from "The Old Country" as they called the U.K.

On Christmas Eve, four of us accepted an invitation to spend the evening with an elderly couple, and when we got there we found a little family of father, mother and two small girls of about seven and nine, had been invited too.

It was a pleasant evening, and when it was time to leave, these young parents invited us to join them on Christmas Day for breakfast and dinner. Acutely aware that our presence would upset their day, we hastily expressed our appreciation of their kind offer, and declined as gracefully as we could. But they would have none of it, and insisted we came. In fact, the two little girls, whom we had spoiled all evening, begged us to accept: we looked furtively at each other and nodded in agreement.

So just before nine next morning we trudged through a heavy wet snow and joined the family.

Their big living room was delightfully warm, and standing out well clear of a corner was a large, decorated Christmas tree. When the two little girls came out, they ran up to us, took us by the hand and asked us to make a circle around the tree. When all eight of us had joined hands, these sweet little souls struck up:-

"*Happy Birthday to you, Happy Birthday to you, Happy Birthday, dear Jesus, Happy Birthday to you.*"

What a lesson it was to us four! We felt greatly humbled.

Have you ever heard of this practice before? And, parents, why not follow their example, next Christmas morning?

Sadly, soon afterwards, we left Canada without a chance to say a last goodbye. A liner had arrived in Halifax, and secretly, in the dead of night, we were called away, back to England and the war.

But it was a Christmas to remember, and all because of two little girls.

Pictures from the past

Gorran Haven about 1889: A photograph taken from the cliff-path to Vault. It shows the Big Cellars, Watch-House, Lime-Kiln, the Ship Inn on the corner (right) and the re-roofed little church of St. Just. Note the washing too, especially on Dick Hennah's hedge. Washing Day was Mondays!

Gorran Haven Harbour 1908: Note that ther are no engines - the old Kelvin had not arrived, so it was 'sail or pull', ie sails or oars. All boats were tarred. When the Kelvins arrived, most of the boats had strakes added to their gunwhales thus spoiling their lines. The bigger crabbers carried up to twenty four '56er's' (half hundredweight weights) for ballast, taken out every night.

Pictures from the past

Gorran Haven today, showing the harbour wall as seen from the Lime-Kiln. A quiet morning at Gorran Haven at half-tide plus, with the Gwineas behind the quay, a mile away. The motley collection of boats contrasts sharply with the tarred crabbers of yesteryear.

Old fishermen at Beach Corner, Gorran Haven circa 1909, Parliament in session. L to R. Fred Ball (father of Charlie), Bill Billing, John Guy (wind up), Richard Rowse, Jimmy Downing (Jnr.), Jimmy Downing, George Liddicoat. (Jessica Johns thinks that the man on the right is Jonny Guy and the third L to R is John Billing: I cannot say who is right.

The new Parliament at beach corner 1925 from the West Briton.
L to R. George Liddicoat, Jacob Billing, Jack Hennah, Charlie Billing, Jack Patten, Edwin Nicholls, William Teague, Nick Liddicoat, George Liddicoat.

Will Pollard with his trammels in his wheelbarrow getting ready for the next morning's 5am start in the Albion. (Circa 1932) Will married a Swiss woman from Berne and they lived in Gorran Haven until they decided to spend their final years among her relatives. Will died in 1990 aged 86 and is buried at Ostermundigen, a suburb of Berne. He was a stalwart of Mount Zion Chapel and his grave is inscribed 'Der Herr ist mein Hirte Ps. 23' (The Lord is my Shepherd).

An early 1930's 'Parliament'. L to R. George Liddicoat, Walter Beer, Edwin Nicholls, William Teague, John Ball, John Coombe, Nick Liddicoat. John Coombe and Nick, sitting beside each other, were incompatible compatibles, good friends but frequently arguing fiercely.

This is a delightful photograph taken in 1937. L to R. Will Dadda, Bob Ball, Pete Billing, and Tommy Kitto. Bob Ball - see 'Dodman's Last Victim', Pete Billing - see 'Heaven on earth by the sea'

Pictures from the past

Bertram Pollard and Will Ball, the last pair of Gorran Haven crabbers from boyhood. These two highly skilled and experienced seamen knew 'all the ground' and marks for a radius of fifteen miles and worked it. Bertram, whose eldest brother Thomas was drowned when his minesweeper blew up in 1917, joined the RAF Air Sea Rescue branch in WW2 and was terribly burned in a fire on board in 1944. I visited him in February, soon after the accident when he was in hospital at Shotley, Co. Durham. He was heavily bandaged from the shoulders up, with only slits for his eyes and mouth. Typical of this lovely man, he gave me a bar of chocolate, his week's ration. I could have wept on the spot and was nearly choked with emotion. He never ceased to be very self-conscious of those disfiguring scars: war is more cruel than the sea. Will Ball was an ideal mate for Bertram, warm, friendly and even-tempered but with high ideals as well, he was an example for all fishermen. He served in minesweepers in WW1, after which Dick Pill built an 18' crabber for him, the Cotswold, named after his last ship, which was scrapped in 1923. This photograph was taken in 1952. The Cotswold is still in Gorran Haven. Geoffrey Fox, the Grandson of Will's brother John, bought it back into the Ball family. Geoff has refitted her and she takes pride of place in the harbour.

Smiles and Tears - Archie Smith *Pictures from the past*

Tommy Billing, Jessica Johns' grandfather in the Melba, circa 1922, with visitors on fishing trip. He knew the precise position of a 'Bib' (Pouting) pit near the Dodman, but would never divulge his secret to anyone. And, that secret died with him. Tommy was about 83 here.

Pictures from the past

This is Dave Patten in the Meta at her moorings in the Inner Tier, circa 1935. His single cylinder Kelvin's box cover is off, and he is cleaning up the plugs ready for the next morning. This is typical Dave's pose. (See 'A sense of humour')

Pipe-laying in Church Street, 1935 for the first sewage scheme. The untreated sewage was discharged at an outfall just beyond Schovella Point in the Pool. Note the gutters and they were slippery! 'Boy' Jacob Billing is the man on the left of the picture. This was a very busy time for our plumbers Jimmy and Ben Holman who lived at the present Mermaid Cafe. When the great day permitting the use of the WCs arrived, there was great excitement, and for several weeks afterwards, Jimmy and Ben went round to check that all was working well. When a dear old soul who had never seen a flush lavatory, was asked how she was getting on, she hesitated and very coyly said, " All right, my dear, but ... I don't like to say it ... every time I use it, it makes my bottom wet. Can'ee do anything 'bout it?" "Yes", said Jimmy in a flash, "I'll fix it for 'ee right away. 'Tis a common fault with these new inventions." So he shortened the chain.

Pictures from the past

Gorran Cricket Team 1st XI, 1954

In 1953 Gorran surprised all those living west of St. Austell when they defeated Falmouth at Penzance by three wickets in the County Senior League final to win the Western Morning News Challenge Cup for the third time. (1937, 1948 and 1953) The selection committee was faced with the age-old dilemma - field the best team available on the day or rely on the team which took them to the final: they chose the former. This is a photograph of the 1953 XI which won the Eastern League, but not all had the glory of playing in the County Final or being photographed with the coveted cup. They are:- L to R, back row. George Burns (umpire), Joe Grose, Harold Bunney, Eric Marks, Tommy Guy, Howard Whetter. Front row. Morley Rowse, Ern Liddicoat, Archie Smith, Leslie Rowse, Jack Hurrell, Freddie Cameron. (only 3 survive today)

Cricket: Gorran's Eastern League winners' cup 1954. Gorran won the coveted Cornwall Senior League cup in 1937, 1948 and 1953. But they also won the Senior League (East) and therefore the runners-up cup in 1950, 1954, 1958, 1963, 1967 and 1972 - an Eastern league record on both counts. I am proudly holding the runners-up cup in 1954 after Gorran's defeat in the final by Penzance.

Pictures from the past

Gorran Church bells were re-hung in 1953

L to R. Rev. J. R. Jose (Vicar), Bobby Tregunna, Foundry-worker, Mrs. Knowles, Laurie Richards (Captain), Les Knowles, Mrs Scoble, Tony Rowse, Hazel Rowse, Tom Hardy, Arthur Scoble, and the Rev. York. These bells were allegedly stolen from Mevagissey and that is why Mevagissey has no church bells - or so "they" say!

The Lynx on trials off the Isle of Wight, and at anchor.(Pictures by kind permission of the National Maritime Museum)

Pictures from the past

HMS Thrasher at anchor, 1896 (Picture by kind permission of National Maritime Museum)

The Katie Cluett, shown at Bridgwater on August 9th 1913. It is easy to imagine that superb bow cutting through the water with the ship in full sail. (Picture by kind permission of National Maritime Museum)

Pictures from the past

From a painting of the Try Again. Just before midnight on 6th October, 1908, William Henry Michell, a farmer who was living at Penare, was aroused by two sailors who, having scaled the cliffs at the Deadman, were seeking help for their critically injured ship's master, Captain J.H. Carbines of St. Ives. He was in command of the Padstow barquentine "Try Again" and she had foundered at the foot of that mighty headland that foggy, stormy night.(Picture by kind permission of the National maritime Museum)

Getting the Mafeking Gun from blacksmith to emplacement.

The unseating of the Hon. T.C.R. Agar-Robartes MP., 1906 "His family had only been characteristically hospitable and asked a few constituents to tea." (Dr. A.L. Rowse)

Pictures from the past

Captain, The Hon. T.C.R. 'Tommy' Agar-Robartes' grave in Lapugnoy Military Cemetery near Bethune, France. The inscription at the base chosen by the family reads:- 'Be thou faithful unto death and I will give thee a crown of life.' (Revelation 2.10)

The original wooden cross which marked Capt. Robartes' grave until 1923, when the Imperial War Graves Commission replaced it. It was brought home to Lanhydrock, encased in glass, and now lies to the South of the Church behind Lanhydrock House.

Photograph of Captain Tommy Robartes taken in 1915 when 'in the field' His friendly, outgoing character is portrayed in his face - even then. (Reproduced by kind permission of the National Trust)

Pictures from the past

Charlie Ball's grave, at Etaples Military Cemetery, France. The wreath reads :- 'To the grandfather I've never met. From your loving granddaughter, Barbara.' (Barbara Palmer, Caerhays)

The grave of Charlie Liddicoat in Wimereux Communal Cemetery, France. It lies flat like all the rest because of the sandy soil. A few paces away lies Lt. Col. John McCrae. Enquiries revealed that Charlie's grave was imminently due for cleaning.

This wreath of poppies, the symbol of Flanders Fields, was laid on behalf of Mayor Joe Young, Mayor of Guelph, Ontario, Canada, the birthplace of John McCrae. That birthplace is now a museum and contains momentoes of him. These include his medals, purchased on Saturday, October 27th, 1997 for the equivalent of £233,000 or C$400,000 (the most expensive ever) by a Canadian who was of Chinese origin. He stunned Canada by giving them to John McCrae's birthplace. This was a manifestation of his gratitude to John McCrae and to his new Country, Canada, as well.

Pictures from the past

John McCrae wrote the immortal poem, which starts 'In Flanders Fields the poppies blow..." (see 'In Flanders Fields they lie together'). Strange is it not that he lies a few yards from Charles Liddicoat, till now just 'somewhere in France'.

Talwyn Oliver at her exhibition, 1997, of her research into her ancestors' fate on the Ypres Front and the Somme, World War 1. Joe Oliver's photograph is on the left of the picture. (see 'the Olivers')

Pictures from the past

The 23 feet high granite Dodman Cross standing defiantly but appealingly high above 'Main Lay', the South Westerly point of the Dodman. Gerrans Bay with its Gull Rock and all the 'Western Land' are clearly visible in the background.

Parson Martin's chosen inscription at the base of the Dodman Cross. This is that godly man's enduring message to all men for all time.

IN THE FIRM HOPE OF THE SECOND COMING OF OUR LORD JESUS CHRIST, AND FOR THE ENCOURAGEMENT OF THOSE WHO STRIVE TO SERVE HIM, THIS CROSS IS ERECTED, A.D. 1896.

The distinctive shape of the Dodman Point at high water, from the Gruda footpath. 'Flat rocks' to the right, then Penveor Cove (beach covered) leading out to Merton (the East-most point) on the left of the picture.

'A sense of humour, a test of sanity'. (Shaw)

A SENSE OF HUMOUR

Gorran men were never in the same class as Mevagissey men when it came to humour. Not that the former were dull, dismal or humdrum, but there never seemed to be the same sense of fun although Gorran men were the equal of all when mischief was involved.

Real humour seemed part of Mevagissey men's lives, especially the fishermen's. Gorran men were dry humoured and they could be less than warm to strangers. For example, on one occasion a car stopped down by the Lime Kiln and the driver, having wound down his window, called out to one of the fishermen leaning against the wall, "Hey, Jack, which is the way to Portloe?"

"Ow did 'ee know me name was Jack?" came the reply.

"Oh, I guessed it," admitted the motorist.

"Well guess yer way to Portloe," was the advice given and he turned away.

On another occasion, a local was walking up by Rice when a car pulled up and the driver, in most courteous terms, asked, "Excuse me, can you please direct me to Truro."

The local paused for a moment and stroked his chin, mumbling to himself, clearly in some difficulty.

"Trura", said he; "well now, let me zee: I tell 'ee if I was 'going to Trura I wouldn't start from 'ere," and that was that.

I have often thought that sixty years ago and more, many of the visitors, who were few in number anyway, were patronising and condescending towards country folk and seemed to think they were ignorant yokels. That would trigger off some fishermen like my grandfather who would seize the opportunity to ask the strangers some question about algebraic formulae and stun them. Others 'knew what the score was' and went along with it or deliberately reinforced the opinions of the visitors. But they could be dry humoured and I was present when one of the biggest ripostes I have ever heard was administered by Boy David Patten. It was in August 1935 or 1936, and Boy Dave was in his crabber the 'Meta' one afternoon when the tide was out and the Meta was aground in the inner tier. It was the usual practice for the fishermen who had a Kelvin Engine to clean the plugs or spit on the cylinder head to keep her in good order. Dave was doing this, the engine cover was off and couple of us were leaning over the gunwale just talking away. Then a visitor and his wife approached, he with white Panama hat and immaculate tropical suit while his wife was equally smartly dressed.

We knew our place and stopped talking, but in any case, our superiors were keen to talk and learn and ignored us. But it didn't take long for us to twig that this gentleman, superior to the three of us in every conceivable way, was not being condescending only, but was 'taking the Mick' out of Dave who in his inimitable way, half smiled. half cackled like a cluck hen as he answered the questions put to him. "And what do you do in the winter time?" he queried with a sort of laugh which suggested that Dave hibernated with the hedgehogs.

"I'll tell 'ee what we do mister," Dave said as he lifted his head and gazed into his superior's face with that half grin, "we de light the vire, pull up the chair and have good old laff as we talk about you crowd who come down 'ere in the summer."

The interview ended and the two visitors melted away. Dave looked at us who had remained speechless, "That was wan for 'un that 'ee didn't expect, wadd'n it?" said he.

It certainly was: and we carried on as if nothing had happened.

But Mevagissey men were past masters at overstatement and my one-time colleague in teaching, Walter John Dunn (Jack) a member of one of the oldest Mevagissey families of shipbuilders and fishermen, was a wonderful raconteur. Indeed, he was also a mimic par excellence and could imitate every inflection of the old men as well as recall their words. Now nearing 90, he has written a book on Mevagissey which is a superb social history as well as an amusing and informative autobiography: I wish someone would publish it for him.

I remember one or two of his tales, all too original to be anything but true.

Dennis Maher was a large, portly man who sported a fine moustache and was the harbour-master. I remember Denny mainly for his ponderous gait and deep, sepulchral voice so I can appreciate Jack's little story.

One day, Denny was 'down quay' on duty and he saw a car approaching. That quay is private property and a charge is levied to park on it or even cross it so Denny walked out into the middle of the quay and stood his ground facing the car. The driver, irritated at this interference with his passage, got out and confronted Denny in a rather aggressive manner. "You have no right to stop me," said he angrily.

Denny drew himself up to his full height, expanded his diaphragm and in that slow, deep bass voice said majestically, "My man, I can not only stop yer car, I can stop yer breath. I'm the harbour-master".

The Mevagissey exaggeration is surely unbeatable. One old chap listened carefully one morning to others talking about their horticultural abilities and the superb things they had grown. When they had done their best, he said, "You lot ain't growed nothing. Wance, I intered the Flower Show and my gooseberries was so big, I could only git three in a pint pot. As fer the cabbage, I could'n get un through the Townhall door."

I think the tallest story of all that Jack told was of the old fisherman sitting 'down quay' one day listening to others talking about rough weather and heavy seas.

He waited patiently without saying a word and when all had said their piece he exclaimed, "You habn' seen notheen. I waz down off the Lizard wance and we zeed a geet zay coming towards us as big as Polkirt Hill and when she went past we wuz left up on top ave 'un, high and dry".

Jack said that the Methodist minister at the time was not to be outdone either. When they were all talking about tiredness on one occasion, the reverend gentleman declared that once he was so tired that when he got up to his bedroom, he took a flying leap and was asleep before his head hit the pillow. Beat that if you can!

The muscles of his brawny arms are strong as iron bands (Longfellow)

A CORNISH INVOLVEMENT IN THE BOER WAR, 1899

Two friends of mine, Sheila and Brian Hammond of St. Austell, have a son who was a member of South Africa's National Chamber Orchestra. During a recent visit to that country, they took the opportunity to visit Mafeking cemetery as Mrs. Hammond's grandfather had taken part in the famous 'Relief of Mafeking' during the Boer War, and they wanted to see the British war graves.

While there, they spotted a granite memorial with the following inscription below the fifteen bezants of the Cornish emblem:-

> In
> Loving Memory
> J. Gerrans
> Born Tregoney, Cornwall
> Died Mafeking
> 2nd June, 1915
> Age 66 years
> 'Now the labourer's task is o'er.'

On their return to Cornwall, they traced him. He was born in the parish of Cuby with Tregony in 1849, was christened Joseph and was baptised on 23rd December, 1849. Still keenly interested, they mentioned this to Dr. David Blight of Sticker, a renowned local historian who informed them that Joseph Gerrans was the man who helped in the making of the famous 'Mafeking Gun', the wheels of which were made from a threshing machine and which is now in the Royal Artillery Museum at Woolwich. He also told them that Joseph Gerrans was joined by a Mr. Truscott from the same area and together they ran a garage in Baden Powell's old Headquarters. These two even organised Motor Trials at Mafeking, involving backing cars into spaces marked out by empty shell cases from the siege. Dr. Blight's cousin Richard Truscott was born in Mafeking in 1932 but the family returned to Cornwall shortly after and kept the Post Office at Tregony.

Intrigued by this fascinating story, I contacted Brigadier Timbers, the

R.A.'s Historical Secretary who sent me the following information about the Mafeking Gun and Joseph Gerrans' involvement:-

'The gun was a 5inch howitzer constructed in the railway workshops at Mafeking. Its barrel was a steel tube strengthened by iron rings shrunk on. It was mounted on a carriage constructed by John Gerrans, a well-known wagon builder in Mafeking, using the wheels of a threshing machine. It did little more than maintain morale in Mafeking by responding to the shelling from the Boers, but a siege morale is an important factor in surviving. After the campaign, the gun was given to Baden-Powell whose nickname was "Wolf" (hence the term Wolf Cubs in the Scouting world). On return to England, he gave the gun to the Queen, and from there it travelled via the R.U.S.I. to Woolwich. It has always been known as the 'Wolf Gun' as a result of that connection.'

As a young cavalry officer Baden-Powell had been sent to Mafeking which he defended. The hero of the relief was Lieut. Col. Plumer who with a thousand men raised in Rhodesia, fought his way down to Mafeking 'with plenty of fighting on the way as well as when we got there'. In the 1914-18 war, Plumer was one of the most successful commanders on the Ypres front, and as Field Marshal Plumer, President of the Ypres League, unveiled the massive MENEN GATE memorial on 27th July, 1927. Later that day, he also laid the foundation stone of St. George's Memorial Church in Ypres.

Gerrans is a most unusual surname and it is highly probable that there was a Gorran connection.

On October 29th, 1793, Tabitha Carveth, who was born in Gorran in 1767, married Thomas Gerrans of Probus at St. Goran. Their son, John Carveth Gerrans was a farmer cum butcher at Lancallan and died there in 1867 aged 71. A Stephen Carveth married Margaret Melhuish at Gorran in 1783 and their daughter Ann married James Billing in 1809 following the death of his first wife Grace Broad in 1808.

All this sounds very complicated but it shows clearly that one does not have to go back more than about two hundred years to find that everybody is related to everyone else in the area.

'Man marks the earth with ruin - his control stops with the shore (Byron)

THE CRUEL SEA

Those who have been brought up by the sea, especially coming from seafaring families, learn from an early age that the sea is no place to fool around. From time to time it has to be faced in its angry mood and that is when the knowledge of the sea, often distilled over many generations, is life-saving. Even then, however, tragedies occur and Gorran Haven has had more than its share over the centuries. Fishermen, often experienced and anything but foolhardy, have on many occasions lost their lives between the Gribben and the Dodman.

One of the worst was on Tuesday, August 9th, 1804. A Gorran Haven seine boat was caught in a sudden violent gale at the Deadman. The seine was precious in the extreme because on it depended the livelihood of the seiners and their families, and their little capital was probably wrapped up in the seine too. Risks might have been unwisely taken, but in the event, John Michell, John Hicks, William Kerkin, William Davis of this parish and Thomas Julian of the parish of St. Breock were drowned.

Jacob Eddy of this parish and Edward Jago of the parish of St. Ewe were thrown on the rocks by the waves and saved.

The Deadman was not so called without reason.

'O hear us when we cry to Thee for those in peril on the sea'. (Wm Whiting)

BRAVERY ON THE DEADMAN AT DEAD OF NIGHT

Shakespeare wrote that 'courage mounteth with occasion', and here is an example.

Just before midnight on 6th October, 1908, William Henry Michell, a farmer who was living at Penare, was aroused by two sailors who, having scaled the cliffs at the Deadman, were seeking help for their critically injured ship's master, Captain J.H. Carbines of St. Ives. He was in command of the Padstow barquentine "Try Again" and she had foundered at the foot of that mighty headland that foggy, stormy night.

One of the Michell family set out at once to summon help from the coastguards, but because of Captain Carbines' plight, the two loyal and brave crewmen asked William Henry if he, being familiar with the cliffs, would lead them down. Without hesitation, he seized ropes and a lantern and set off. It is not an easy descent even in broad daylight; at night, in fog and wet, it was daunting in the extreme. William Henry led the two sailors safely down to the rocks using ropes in perilous places, and secured the injured captain who happened to be a big, heavy man. Inch by inch he was brought to the summit which was not reached till first light and from there he was taken to the Michells' farm at Penare where he remained for several weeks until able to be moved.

William Henry's youngest son Walter, was ten years of age at the time and remembered the drama vividly, according to his son Leonard who now lives on the Isles of Scilly.

There's a happy ending to this ship-wreck. Although the "Try Again" was lost, Captain Carbines recovered and some time later, William Henry received a letter requesting him to present himself at Buckingham Palace as His Majesty, King Edward VII wished to present him personally with a medal 'in recognition of his selfless courage and gallant conduct during this hazardous rescue'. It took place on November 8th, 1908.

The medal passed to William Henry's eldest son, Herbert, and is now in the possession of his daughter Marjorie.

'Courage mounteth with the occasion' indeed!

When the Gorran Haven coastguards were alerted, they hastened to the scene to help in the hazardous climb up the cliff with the heavy Captain Carbines. Chief Officer Tyson was later commended for his assistance.

THE DODMAN'S LAST VICTIM

The last victim of the Dodman was a three-masted schooner of 130 tons gross and ninety four feet long called the Katie Cluett. She was built in Fowey at the yard of a John Stephens at Caffa Mill, just upstream from the Bodinnick Ferry slip-way, in 1876. She was renowned along the south coast for her speed and her graceful lines and she was said to be the fastest of them all. Her first owner was a Liskeard merchant but she was eventually bought by Captain Alfred Prettyman of Pentewan and others.

The Prettymans were a distinguished seafaring family which hailed from Yarmouth, on the East coast. James Prettyman, a sailor, moved to Pentewan where he started a coal business and chandlery in 1860. He had six sons, James, Archie, Stanley, George, Alfred and Ernest, all of whom went to sea. Four of these became masters of vessels while the other two were ships' engineers. The four masters either owned their vessels or shared with another famous Pentewan ship-broker, Charles P. Couch, who incidentally did not retire until 1960.

Alfred became the part owner and master of the Katie Cluett, and traded not only around British waters, but also overseas, making many voyages to Newfoundland engaged in the salt fish trade.

On Christmas Eve, 1917, according to his nephew, Geoffrey Prettyman who still lives at Pentewan, the Katie Cluett was in convoy heading for Falmouth which was reached late on December 23rd. It was dark and a strong East South East wind was blowing with heavy sea running. The convoy broke up at Falmouth but Cap'n Alf decided to make for home. Some time after midnight on the 23rd the Katie Cluett ran ashore on the Dodman. The precise time - and indeed the details of the wreck - are uncertain because of conflicting reports. One member of the crew of four said it was 1.00 am and another 4.00 am. The former is most likely correct as the Mevagissey lifeboat was called out at 4.00 am., before which a survivor had to climb the cliff and raise the alarm. A press report states that nearly all the members of the two regular lifeboat crews were either away on service with the Forces or at the Plymouth herring fishery, so a volunteer crew mustered and launched the boat. They found that the vessel had been totally lost in the gale. Those who know the Dodman in an E.S.E. gale will also know that the life-boat could not have rendered any assistance in any case.

Somehow, three members of the crew managed to get ashore and climbed the cliff. The coastwatcher on duty at the look-out hut that night was 'Bob' Ball, a Gorran Haven fisherman. In the early hours he was startled to hear a hammering on the door followed by the mate Richard Richards bursting in to raise the alarm. Bob immediately called out the Mevagissey life-boat and the coast-guards, but neither could be of help.

When dawn broke on Christmas Eve, the Katie Cluett, with her square rigged foremast sails still in place, lay hard and fast right under the cliff, on the East side by Merton Rock, in the Gallowses area.

The body of Cap'n Alf could not be found but within a day or so, the wind turned South West enabling Gorran men to get down to the wreck in their boats. Two days later, a Gorran Haven fisherman, 'Johnny' Coombe, managed to clamber down between a cleft in the rocks at low tide and found the body of the master.

At the inquest the reason for Cap'n Alf's loss was never determined. One report was that he had got ashore and was seen on a rock by a survivor while another thought he had gone back to help another member of the crew whom he thought was still aboard. Clearly, he had gone back for some reason and thereby lost his life.

He was buried in St. Austell Cemetery 'in the presence of a large gathering' on the following Saturday afternoon and left a widow and a daughter. The Coroner, Mr. Carlyon, recorded a verdict of "Accidental drowning, as decided by a jury".

Two residents of Gorran Haven, Mr. Lewis Billing and Mrs. Jessica Johns (née Billing) now in their late eighties clearly remember the tragedy. Lewis's grandfather, William Robert Billing (Billy Bob) took Lewis and 'Boy Jim' Liddicoat out to see the wreck, and his grandfather got some canvas from her for a mizzen and a mainsail. Henry Hill, Lewis recalls, retrieved the heavy iron ring-shaped fitting into which the top mast slotted, and this he used for a mooring for his boat. Lewis reckons it is still down there somewhere!

Jessica has vivid memories of being taken down to Vault and out to Penveor by her grandfather Tommy. Accompanied by Ena Ball (afterwards Ena Prynn) her friend, they picked up a few toys, presumably meant for the children of the crew and which were floating in one of the little inlets by Penveor Cove. Lewis also recalls that as the Katie Cluett was in ballast, there was but little to salvage. However, the masts were valuable and these, he said, were pulled out and towed away by a tug from Falmouth.

My father, a regular Royal Navy man, had been serving on the battlecruiser Inflexible for the past five years and she 'paid off' just before Christmas. This allowed him to have the first Christmas at home since 1911. He became engaged to my mother on Christmas Eve and they went down to Vault Beach to see the wreck in the afternoon. Washed up on the foreshore was a drowned rooster, another pathetic reminder of the tragic early hours.

It is unlikely that the Katie Cluett will ever be forgotten in Gorran Haven because 1917 was the blackest year in the history of this little fishing village. Five young men at war had already lost their lives on land or sea during those fateful months, and Cap'n Alf Prettyman's loss on Christmas Eve while his wife and daughter waited for him, completed the year of tragedy and sorrow.

'The cliffs of England stand glimmering and vast out in the tranquil bay'. (Matthew Arnold)

A NAVAL TRAGEDY, 100 YEARS AGO

In 1866, an Englishman named Robert Whitehead, invented a 'vehicle' which could travel a short distance under water at about six knots.

Two years later, he put a warhead on it and the torpedo, named after an electric ray which stuns its prey, was born. It was an invention which was to change the course of naval warfare: all other craft would be vulnerable to it. Much alarmed, the Admiralty developed craft capable of carrying these torpedoes, naming them Torpedo Boats, but also sought craft to combat them.

As the Torpedo Boats were light and fast, the 'Catchers', as they were called, had to be faster still. In fact, by the mid 1890s, the Navy had ordered a number of '30 knotters' as they were called. All these vessels were of flimsy construction with plates about the thickness of strong cardboard. They 'panted' and crew conditions were so cramped and uncomfortable that the men were given a special allowance, 'hard-lying'. It was said that if these 'Catchers', later named Torpedo Boat Destroyers', and later still 'Destroyers', were involved in a collision, they would fold up like a concertina. This proved to be true as we shall see.

On the 29th September, 1897, three destroyers, the SUNFISH, THRASHER and the LYNX left St. Ives soon after midnight on a training exercise. Apparently they ran into fog somewhere around the Longships and eased down, continuing up channel at reduced speed. Presumably they were on 'dead reckoning' so their precise whereabouts was not known but by mid-morning they found out - two of them hit the Dodman.

The following is a unique record of this tragedy, taken from the diary of a former Mevagissey fisherman, Ambrose Pollard, whose father of the same name was the first man to reach the stricken vessels and related the story to him. I am indebted to Mr. Geoffrey Pollard for permitting me to extract it from his father's diary and to have it printed.

'The date was 29th September, 1897. There was a dense fog with hardly any wind and the "Percy" (PERSEVERANCE) was just making headway South West of the Dodman with both sails set - the 120 yard foresail and the 80 yard mizzen. The crew were taking turns at rowing with the large sweeps as the little wind was

southerly. There was one man forward on the lookout, and he suddenly thought he could hear the sound of steam escaping on the port bow. The crew members stopped rowing, and my father, who was steering at the time, put the helm to starboard and made for the sound. It was getting louder every minute and they could also hear the sound of men's voices as if in distress. Father had by this time lowered the sails and they all rowed towards the sound. It was not long before a large object loomed up, and when they came close enough, to their surprise and dismay found that it was H.M.S. THRASHER of our Navy which had been on trials with the LYNX and the SUNFISH. The SUNFISH had eased speed and saw the steep cliffs in time. She went full astern, hove about and made for Falmouth. LYNX and THRASHER had not eased down till too late and crashed on to the dreaded Dodman. The LYNX managed to kedge herself off and limped back to Plymouth, but the THRASHER was not so fortunate. The impact on striking the rocks fractured the main steam pipe and clouds of steam burst into the boiler room. Three men escaped up the ladders but three others were trapped inside. One crew member, an Irish stoker named Lynch, fought his way down below and dragged out a stoker named Paul. Both were severely scalded but poor Lynch who was taken to the home of a coastguard, died that same evening. The other two stokers also died.

Father's boat took off some of the crew members with some of their personal belongings and went to Falmouth. One officer gave my father a pair of binoculars as a keepsake and the Admiralty gave the crew four pounds each, paid in sovereigns, for their assistance.

The next day an Admiralty tug towed the THRASHER off and to Falmouth where temporary repairs were made, enabling her to reach Devonport, and after being of good service in the 1914-18 war, she was broken up in 1921.'

Stoker Lynch's heroism is still remembered and honoured by the indigenous population of Gorran Haven. My father, who was eleven years of age at the time, told me that when he was brought ashore, Stoker Lynch's skin 'was hanging off in ribbons'.

Some time later Stoker Lynch was posthumously awarded the Albert Medal, an award instituted in 1866. The criteria for this award was:- 'Heroic acts performed by mariners and others who endanger their own lives in saving, or endeavouring to save the lives of others from shipwrecks and other perils of the sea'.

The Albert Medal was replaced by the George Cross in 1971 although recipients of the former could exchange their award for a George Cross if they chose to do so.

N.B. The Perseverance, a Lugger, was built at Gorran Haven by Dick Pill and Gorran men helped in the rescue. They too were paid in sovereigns.

The Thrasher and the Lynx went ashore in the 'Bell' the central part of the headland between Main Lay on the West side and Gallowses on the East. There is deep water in the Bell and close in, so there was no stranding on submerged rocks: they were fortunate.

Lift high his Royal Banner. (George Duffield)

THE DODMAN CROSS

The Dodman, or the Deadman as locals always called it, is one of the dominant features of Cornwall's South coast. For centuries, sailors approaching our shores as they battled their way up Channel, peered into the distance for the first sight of land - and all knew the Deadman.

They avoided it at all costs, but used it to take their bearings and set course for their home port.

Even in the early days of World War 2, German bombers used it to pinpoint their exact position on moonlight or daylight sorties from their bases in France.

On the top of the Dodman's western tip, 373 feet above the sea, stands the Dodman Cross, the story of which is most interesting.

It was built in 1896 by the Rev. George Martin, then Rector of Caerhayes. He was a deeply religious, godly man who each day sought the remoteness of the great promontory to commune with his Lord, and pray. In some respects, he was like Parson R.S. Hawker, Vicar of Morwenstow, an eccentric who loved above all to walk along those high and foreboding cliffs of North Cornwall to a little hut in the cliff top where he too, could contemplate.

Mr. Fred Michell, now ninety years of age, farmed at Boswinger all his life and he clearly remembers his father, Mr. Edward Michell who was born in 1866, talking about Rev. Martin who passed through the farm each time and knew him well. He told young Fred that the Rector wanted that cross to be the first thing that sailors saw when they sighted land - the symbol of Jesus Christ and Calvary.

In her book 'Schoolhouse in the Wind', Anne Treneer, whose father was the headmaster of Gorran School and later moved to Caerhayes School wrote:

'The arms of the cross stood across the sky - a powerful symbol. We were awed by it. George Martin had the cross set up. He would come to us for all kinds of meals, especially breakfast after spending the night on Dodman.'

The Dodman had a curious attraction for Anne. The last time I saw her was right there late on a September evening as the full moon shed its silvery light over the western bay towards the Lizard: we were both enchanted by the scene below us.

When one considers George Martin, his faith, his humility and his devotion to his Master, it comes as no surprise to read the inscription at the base of his cross. It was undoubtedly chosen with great care and reads:

'In the firm hope of the second coming of our Lord Jesus Christ and for the encouragement of those who serve Him. This cross is erected A.D. 1896.'

The Dodman now belongs to the National Trust and has a good carpark at Penare. No visit to South Cornwall is complete without a visit to the Cross in the footsteps of that saintly rector over a century ago: it is an unforgettable experience.

'Let another's shipwreck be your seamark' (17th Century Proverb)

THE LOSS OF THE ARDANGORM

The story of the Ardangorm has never been told before. No doubt in archives somewhere her loss was recorded, but I have not been able to find it. Indeed, few people will have even heard her name and the reason is not hard to find.

During wartime, any information which might in any way, have been construed as of 'use to the enemy' was censored. There were no newspaper reports or anything else; the name, her fate were shrouded in silence.

This comparatively detailed record has been made possible by three people who have willingly and without question given me every assistance.

I therefore acknowledge access to the diary of the late Ambrose Pollard who crewed with Preston Thomas during the salvage operations, and I am most grateful to his son, Geoffrey for the privilege. I am also particularly grateful to Arthur Frazier, William's son, who allowed me to talk to him for two hours on end and whose memory of all the events is still crystal clear. He is known as 'memory man', an apt description indeed.

Lastly, I thank Mrs. June Ford (née Thomas) daughter of Preston who was so important to the salvaging of the wrecked vessel.

Not least in her memory is the visit to her father, when at home, by Customs Officers, who were trying to trace some liquor which had been spirited away by someone. Her father was affronted; no Mevagissey man would dream of that! And I can vouch for Gorran men as no boat had been launched. There were many gremlins in war-time!

Soon after darkness had fallen on the night of Thursday, January 4th, 1940, Gorran Haven's two zealous Air-Raid Wardens, Matt Brown and Tom Addy, put on their greatcoats and warm headgear before venturing out to check on the efficiency of householders' blackouts. Any chink of light caused them to knock on the door and gently but firmly remind those inside of this serious breach of regulations.

A cold South-East wind made the raw January night even colder, and the 'Easterly rattle' of the sea was the only sound to be heard: the scene was dismal. As the villagers crept up their stairs to bed, a 5,200 ton Glasgow registered ship was making her way up Channel, bound for Fowey from Canada and in ballast. The wind out there was strong E.S.E. and her course was set N.E. so the wind was catching her starboard side. Little did the ship's master realise that she was making leeway because the wind was stronger than that in his dead-reckoning calculations, there being no other navigational help in those days. As the Ardangorm approached her estimated time of arrival at Fowey, several eyes peered into the darkness for some sign of land as there was concern about her true position. Suddenly, a look-out on the bridge thought he could see land on the port bow and the helmsman heaved the wheel to starboard to make for the open sea, but in a short time she was hard and fast on the Eastern (far) side of the Gwineas and parallel to it: she would never move again except downwards. Ironically, there is deep water inside the Rock (as locals always called the Gwineas) as well as deep water on the Chapel Point side and fairly deep water to the South towards the present bell-buoy, but on the East side, as far as the treacherous Yaw and beyond, it is shallow and should be avoided.

The light sleepers in Gorran Haven were awakened by the sounding of a ship's siren for some time, but when it stopped, they went back to sleep. Meanwhile, however, the Fowey lifeboat had been alerted and raced to the scene to take off the crew. When daylight appeared, the reason for the ship's siren was apparent - the Rock was almost dwarfed by a big vessel aground behind it. Her stern was towards Chapel Point and her bow faced South East, opposite the intended direction. It would appear that she came well inside the Rock, and the land spotted may well have been Penamaen Point!

Action was swift. The owners sold the wreck to a firm of shipbreakers in Southampton - Risdon Beazley - and they engaged Willie Frazier, a Mevagissey boat-builder to remove whatever could be salvaged. He came from a line of ship-builders. and his yard, not big enough for large craft, was ideal for the construction of yachts and fishing boats, especially the famous 'Toshers'. It was located at the eastern end of the North pier, opposite 'jetty head', and Willie was a particularly highly skilled organiser.

There were two separate parts to this salvage operation, one being the recovery of whatever equipment could be dismantled and brought ashore, and the other was the more important - the recovery of the gun which was fixed near the stern with its barrel looking aft. It was a 4.5 inch gun, manned by Naval gunners and was of the type used on merchant vessels as a means of defence. But in an attack on a convoy, or if the ship was attacked when sailing out of convoy, it was a help. These guns came under the control of the Admiralty and within days, three men in Naval uniform appeared at the door to Willie Frazier's little office to discuss the operation and terms.

Willie had already surveyed the Ardangorm's position and condition, so his plan was ready for every part of the salvage operation. He put Alf Cloke, an experienced and skilled shipwright in charge of the equipment salvaging, and hired the tosher JUELEN and its owner Preston Thomas to do the 'ferrying'. Preston engaged another experienced seaman and fisherman Ambrose Pollard as his mate, and all was ready. It was an astute move. The Juelen had been built by Willie and his men to the specification of Preston in 1939 - even to the exact shade of green! She was the first of the larger toshers, 23 feet long and a much admired little craft.

Alf's team removed as much of the equipment aboard as they could, all in order of value, and the Juelen brought it into Mevagissey harbour where it was transferred to Keir's garage until taken by lorry to the Customs office in Fowey, but what about the gun?

A 4.5 inch naval gun had a barrel sixteen feet long and without its breech, weighed two tons and two hundredweights. It was no peashooter! The naval contingent were anxious to know how Willie was going to get it from the Ardangorm to the jetty and suggested he got a lighter from Fowey. But he would have none of that, and said bluntly that the Juelen would do it with no problems. Much taken aback, they offered £150 for a successful salvage with the gun on the quay, but insisted 'no gun, no payment' - not a penny even to compensate for any losses of block and tackle, hawsers etc.; the deal was struck.

The Juelen was specially adapted for the excessive load, and the gun was removed to the starboard quarter, even though the Ardangorm listed to port. This was essential to permit the stricken craft to afford some protection when the Juelen came alongside. Luck was with Willie and his team; the sea went down almost to a dead calm, and all was made ready with Willie directing operations. The plan was that the gun should be lowered inch by inch with the Juelen positioned perfectly below. The great danger lay with the slight motion of the tide which caused the Juelen to rise and fall. Should the gun be let go too soon or when the boat was down it would go right through her. All waited with bated breath and with Willie concentrating on the precise moment to shout "Let go!" It came exactly, at the right second. The gun was safely aboard, Mevagissey here we come! All this happened in mid-afternoon and I was on my way home to Silver Seas at the time, when to my utter astonishment, I looked out towards 'Rock' and saw this green tosher slowly but surely making her way in a dead calm sea towards Chapel Point. The Juelen was down a bit by the head, and the barrel protruded way beyond the bow. I doubt if any aboard dared to cough, but she rounded Chapel Point and landed the gun. Willie got his £150 and all his team shared in the time-honoured way - i.e. each according to his role. Arthur and fellow apprentices received £17/10/0 each - a small fortune to them at the time. But it was the pride of achievement which they all treasured most.

The salvaged equipment was sold by auction and Willie Frazier bought the second officer's desk for his wife. In due time, this fell to Arthur to whom the timber in it was more valuable than the desk itself, and it was used thus.

The story does not quite end there. Local fishermen say that 'white water' or a dead calm is always blown away by an East wind. And so it was that January. Late on a Friday night, it sprang up from due East, and hard. The Ardangorm, her back already broken was broadside on to the waves and began to settle. Everything which remained on deck had to remain except that which washed ashore - straight into Gorran Haven between the quay and Perhaver Point. An inveterate wrecker, I was soon down there to be joined by Frank Guy on my far right. I went for hatch covers and retrieved eight, all in perfect condition. I wheeled these to my allotment at Parc an Gates with a view to making the strongest hens' house of all time as they must have been about three inches thick at least. But alas, my carpentry skills were never called for; someone stole them and I never saw them again. The Ardangorm was gradually swallowed up by the sea and only the great boilers remained by the end of the war. Today, they are covered in seaweed.

Frank Guy may have a memento, but I have memories.

N.B. The record of the National Maritime Museum is as follows:-

'The Ardangorm was built in 1930 and there was one sister ship. She was the only Connell built vessel owned by the Ardan Steamship Co. Ltd., whose managers were Clark and Service.'

Sorrow ends not when it seemeth done (Shakespeare's Richard II)

WORLD WAR TWO - FORCES' KILLED, GORRAN PARISH

At the Remembrance Day service at the Gorran Parish Church on Sunday, 14th November 1996 a plaque was dedicated to the memory of the five men of this Parish who lost their lives in World War II. Four of the men were members of His Majesty's Armed Forces and the fifth was a civilian, acting as a coast-watcher at Hemmick.

The delay of half a century in carrying out this little act of remembrance may be seen by some as a sad reflection on previous Parish Councils but this would be unfair. The number is inscribed on our War Memorial but somehow or other, until recently, no one seems to have noticed that there is, on the north wall in the church itself, a roll of honour of those lost in World War I but none for World War II. As soon as the Parish Council were made aware of this, they immediately took steps to rectify the omission.

The five names appearing on the scroll are:-

W/O GERALD ROBERT JAMES DAVIS	R.A.F.
LDG/SEAMAN DESMOND GEORGE DOWDING	R.N.
LT. RICHARD FITZGERALD LILLEY	ROYAL ENGINEERS
LT. RONALD JELLETT LILLEY	ROYAL ARTILLERY
ERNEST JOHN OLIVER	COAST-WATCHER

I knew them all, so I am able to write a short account of each (Ernest's story, see 'the Olivers').

Gerald was the son of Amy Davis of Gorran High Lanes and the brother of Monica who lives at Tregerrick. As a boy he attended Gorran School before going on to St. Augustine's, Slough and St. Boniface's College, Plymouth. At the age of 17 1/2 he joined the Royal Air Force and trained as a Wireless Operator/Observer, a specialist for twin-engined bombers.

In 1940 he was posted to 203 Squadron, Coastal Command, and was further posted to the Middle East. His last footstep on his native soil was at St. Eval when he stepped into a Blenheim and navigated her to Gibraltar. After completing his operational tour, he was posted back to the U.K. by ship, there being an acute shortage of aircraft returning. Due to intense enemy submarine activity, the ship was routed via the Cape. Twice she was forced to return to port as the convoy broke up. On the third attempt she was torpedoed and Gerald was lost, presumed killed, on September 12th, 1942, aged 22. He has no known grave but is commemorated by name on Column 249 of the Alamein Memorial, Egypt, along with 11,873 soldiers and airmen who have no known grave.

Gerald was a quiet, fair-haired studious lad who was incapable of offending anyone. His loss was deeply felt locally, though few knew other than he was serving as R.A.F. aircrew.

Desmond was the son of Harry Fred Dowding and of Eleanor Dowding, and brother of Clifford. His father served with the Royal Navy and after retirement joined the Coastguard Service and was posted to Gorran Haven. Desmond attended Gorran School and then joined the Royal Navy as a boy entrant. He was an intelligent, conscientious and personable young man and he was hoping for a commission when he was drafted to the battleship H.M.S. Barham. He was lost in her on November 25th, 1941, aged 22, when she was torpedoed in the Mediterranean. The Barham is a war grave, but Desmond is remembered on the Plymouth Naval Memorial, on Panel 45, Column 3.

Richard and Ronald were the second and third sons of Eric Gordon Lilley and Anne Janet Lilley of Trewollock Lane, Gorran Haven. They received a public school education and Ronald was a scholar at Corpus Christi College, Cambridge. They spent their holidays at Gorran Haven together with their eldest brother Gordon. They had a boat but their great love was cricket. Richard was an excellent all-rounder and a classic front-foot attacking batsman. Ronald had remarkable double-jointed wrists and could bend the hands back so that his fingers touched his wrists. He had no difficulty in bowling leg-breaks, top-spinners and googlies, all of which cause most men to nearly twist their arms off. Apart from everything else, Gorran Cricket Club lost two young players of outstanding promise when they were killed.

Richard was killed in the Normandy Campaign on August 4th, 1944 and is buried in the Bayeux War Cemetery, Plot 15, Row L, Grave 4. He was 22. Ronald was killed in the push across Northern Germany on March 24th, 1945, just six weeks before the war ended. He was aged 21 and he is buried in the Reichwald War Cemetery, Cleves, Plot 53, Row B, Grave 17. Their brother Gordon was called back from the front lest the Lilleys lost all three sons.

> *"They shall not grow old as we that are left grow old;*
> *Age shall not weary them, nor the years condemn,*
> *At the going down of the sun and in the morning*
> *We will remember them".*

If you have tears, prepare to shed them now (Shakespeare - Julius Caesar)

IN FLANDERS FIELDS THEY LIE TOGETHER

One of the sixteen Gorran men who died in World War I was Charles Liddicoat, son of Nicholas and Sarah Liddicoat who lived a few yards from Beach Corner at Gorran Haven.

Called to the colours in 1916, he was drafted to the Duke of Cornwall's Light Infantry and, in due course, to the battlefields of the Somme.

In one bitter and protracted engagement in 1917, he was severely wounded and spent four days in a shell-hole before his comrades got him back to a field dressing station. A Medical Officer at the time sent in this report:-

'One man was brought in who had been lying in no-man's land for some days. He had compound fractures of both legs and I had to give him chloroform to splint them straight enough to allow the stretcher to get through the communication trench. When he came round, I tried to give him some brandy. He rounded fiercely on me and said, "How dare you give me that: I've been a teetotaller all my life". It might have been Charlie.

Charlie died of those wounds on November 7th, 1917, and was buried in Wimereux Communal Cemetery in France with other victims of the Somme including nurses and medical staff whose compassion had taken them into the jaws of hell.

And in that lonely grave he has lain ever since - lamented but unvisited.

His niece Vera Fowler (née Liddicoat) contacted me and asked if I could trace him when I visited the Somme. I did; it was a moving experience.

Like all the rest, Charlie's headstone lies flat because of the sandy soil which will not allow the headstones to stay vertical.

On behalf of our village, I placed a wreath on the grave and took a few paces back to reflect.

There beneath me was the grave of Lt. Col. John McCrae, Canadian Army Medical Crops who died of pneumonia in January, 1918. Born in Guelph, Ontario, he had taken part in the relief of Mafeking, but at the outbreak of the 1914-18 war, he enlisted in the Canadian Expeditionary Force as a medical officer. He went through the horrors of the Ypres salient before being appointed Senior Medical Officer of a huge field hospital near Etaples which dealt with the casualties of the Somme. Due to long exposure to the elements as well as to suffering and warfare itself, he developed pneumonia and died. On his death-bed, he asked to be taken to a place where he could look out over the English Channel towards his homeland; this was granted.

I wonder if perchance he tended to the wounds of poor Charlie and I wonder too if Charlie looked out over the Channel and sighed for home. We shall never know, but we do know that John McCrae and Charlie lie together in that foreign field.

John McCrae?

While in Flanders, he wrote that immortal poem, the simplest and most poignant of all war poems. You will know it:-

In Flanders' Fields

In Flanders' fields the poppies blow
Between the crosses, row on row,
That mark our place; and in the sky
The larks, still bravely singing, fly
Scarce heard amid the guns below.
'We are the dead. Short days ago
We lived, felt dawn, saw sunset glow,
Loved and were loved, and now we lie
In Flanders' fields

Take up the quarrel with the foe;
To you from failing hands we throw
The torch; be yours to hold it high.
If ye break faith with us who die
We shall not sleep, though poppies
Grow in Flanders' fields.

As one looks out over cemetery after cemetery of soldiers' graves in countless thousands, one is filled with a sense of helplessness besides sadness. We can no longer take up the quarrel with the foe.

I particularly like the following lines from Longfellow, who recaptures for all visitors to Flanders, Ypres - indeed, any war cemetery - that

soul searching guilt and sorrow.
In his case it was the grave of an unknown soldier.

'Thou unknown hero sleeping by the sea
In thy forgotten grave; with secret shame
I feel my pulses beat, my forehead burn.
When I remember what thou has given for me -
All that thou hadst, thy life, thy very name,
And I can give thee nothing in return.'

'One woe doth tread upon another's heel, So fast they follow.' (Shakespeare's Hamlet)

THE OLIVERS

Having been brought up between the two world wars, I was never far removed from the horrors of warfare, especially of those ghastly trenches of the Somme and Flanders. My father served every day of that first war - and, as it eventually happened, every day of the second world war too - so memories and mementoes were ever before me. But not only so: I saw legless men hobbling around on crutches, a shell-shocked man with a large black beard roaming the roads, and above all, war widows in black: all intrigued me. I asked questions - who, where, what and so on as well as why - but somehow or other these questions were side-stepped rather than answered: it was one way of protecting us from the truth.

Perhaps the catalyst which was to haunt me happened in the middle to late 1930s when Hitler had come to power and there was widespread speculation about his intentions in Europe. Our 'parliament' at Beach Corner were prophets of doom and at the end of one of these debates, John Vercoe, who was sitting on the 'Bock' beside me, became unusually agitated and launched out. It was clear that the talk had triggered his memory of the horrible experiences he had lived through at Passchendaele, memories he had been desperately trying to forget. I sat spell-bound and shocked as he recalled falling back in the face of a sudden German onslaught, digging in and breaking off the bones of buried comrades around which the putrid, rotting flesh still hung.

Little wonder that when September 3rd, 1939 came and we were at war with Germany once again, nothing else mattered to me.

'Our war', as my generation called it, though just as brutal and dehumanising, could never equal those unspeakable horrors of the trenches of world war one unless we included Belsen and the evil concentration camps. Our fighting forces were cosseted in comparison. Throughout my four years in the R.A.F. I always slept in a bed and between sheets. The 'night-flying suppers' given to aircrew were two-course meals never seen elsewhere. In truth, when one looks back at those days, one cannot but feel guilty, indeed speechless, when the poor lads of the Flanders fields are brought back to mind.

My wife's father was one of the first casualties at Ypres and never recovered fully from head wounds. He had seen the Cloth Hall in all its glory before being destroyed and longed to see it again after being rebuilt. Even after 'our war' was over, I was still drawn to those poor men who in their countless thousands, lay buried in neat rows, acre after acre, in foreign fields.

One day a few years ago, I attended a funeral in St. Goran Church and sat beneath the bronze plaque towards the rear and fixed to the North wall. Once again I read the names of the fallen and pondered as I awaited the mournful voice of the vicar as the cortege approached the South door. It suddenly occurred to me that the number of names on that plaque was three less than the figure inscribed on the war memorial beyond the Lych gate. Why this discrepancy and who were they? The search lasted nearly three years during which time despair set in more than once but success came eventually through a chance remark. It did not take me long to deduce that the missing names were Olivers.

This is one of the oldest families in Gorran Parish. Nicholas Oliver was named in the Protestation Returns for Gorran in 1641. When the Poll Tax was levied in the 17th Century, and imposed on people over sixteen years, 'Edward Oliver and wife' and 'John Oliver' were among those listed in Gorran. And ever since, the Olivers, variously farmers, fishermen, coopers, carpenters, grocers, tailors and dressmakers, have appeared in Gorran records. In the 1881 census, eighteen are recorded: they were a big family.

They were also religious, ardent Dissenters. The Trust Deed of Mt. Zion Congregational Chapel dated 24th January, 1863 shows that five of the eight Trustees (all men) were Olivers. One of the tenets firmly held by members of Mt. Zion, was 'predestination and election of grace', a factor which I believe lay behind the omission of those names on the plaque in the Church.

The facts are that when war broke out in 1914, there were three Olivers who were liable for War Service - Will, Joseph and Courtney. Will was a carpenter with shipwright skills and his skills were needed so he was posted as a civilian/dockyard worker to Scotland and Rosyth. While there, he was required to work on a ship which had docked with fever aboard and he was one who contracted it and died.

Joe was called up for the Army and was posted to the Hampshire Regiment. He was killed on 20th September, 1917.

Courtney, posted to the Royal Engineers was killed on November 28th, 1917 - just two months after Joe.

All three of this close-knit family were gone.

My family, the Teagues, were closely connected with the Olivers and I often enquired about the war dead of the village but I could never get anything but scant information. My mother's first cousin, Thomas Pollard was one, and all I ever got was that he was drowned when his minesweeper blew up, and 'Aunt Fanny had never been the same since'. Of the Olivers, I learned less, only, that the little dinghy in the rafters above the Olivers' shed at Liberty belonged to Courtney, and Lina, a cousin to whom he was engaged, would never allow it to be moved again.

The mystery was compounded when in 1996, I asked the few survivors of this nearly died-out family if they had any information or knowledge about those three. Curiously there was not a shred - no number, no rank, no name, no regiment - nothing.

Why? It is true that 1917 was a terrible year for the Parish; John Charles Kerkin, Charlie Ball, Charlie Liddicoat, William Henry Patten, Joe Oliver, Thomas Pollard, Courtney Oliver - were all lost. The people were devastated, indeed pulverised and may well have been too shocked to mourn or think; we shall never know.

But what about those Oliver omissions? Perhaps the family could never accept that God had permitted those young men to be cut off just like the rest yet the fact was that they were dead. It was a dilemma indeed. Their faith held, but they remained silent and, apparently, destroyed everything associated with that war.

The key to the mystery surrounding the fate of these Olivers was a note sent to me by a local researcher, Christine Hammond. On a grave in Gorran Churchyard was the headstone of Mary Jane Oliver who died in 1914 and underneath her name were the words:- Also in memory of her beloved youngest son, Joseph, killed in France 20th September, 1917 aged 21 years.

I was eventually able to trace his grave - not in France but Belgium.

He was posted to the Hampshire Regiment and was killed near Ypres, not far from Hellfire Corner . He is buried in Larchwood (Railway Cuttings) cemetery.

Courtney was traced to a company of the Royal Engineers. He was killed on November 28th, 1917, near Cambrai in that great tank battle. He has no known grave but is commemorated on the walls of the Louverval Memorial, West of Cambrai.

But this is not the end of the story.

When World War 2 started in September 1939, there was only one young Oliver - Ernest John, son of Elsie and John. The latter farmed Rice, together with some acres near Penhall, and as he was of retiring age though still active, the family decided John should do so in favour of young Ernest. The thought of losing the last of the Olivers was unbearable so Ernest took over. However, he was still required to do some War Service - Home Guard or Coastwatching - so he chose the latter. Alas, while on duty at Hemmick one night in 1941, a lone German bomber for some reason jettisoned its bombs, killing Ernest and a soldier near him. How cruel can fate be, if there be such a thing as fate?

Ernest married a short time before he took over Rice and his wife Dora was pregnant when that bomb fell. Despite the terrible shock, she braved it all and did not lose the baby. That child was a boy who was named Ernest, like his father. He inherited his father's artistic talents and has recently retired as Head of Art at Torquay Grammar School. Today, he is the Chairman of the Gorran Haven Fishermen's Society and has a home in the village too.

That is not the end of the story either. I felt compelled to find the Olivers' graves, leave a wreath on each and photograph them, which I did. Ernest was so touched by these memories, that he took off for France and Belgium and paid homage himself to those forgotten relatives. But it did not stop there either! Ernest's daughter Talwyn, became intrigued with her father's enthusiasm and caught it. She persuaded him to take her to Flanders and the Somme where she and her father made incredible forays into all the war areas of their forebears.

Talwyn chose to do a dissertation on her researches as part of her finals in her degree course. I have read this dissertation: it is a masterly effort.

But what I find so very rewarding is that this young woman to whom 'my war' is almost ancient history, should be able to empathise so totally with those thousands of soldiers who lie in Flanders fields.

Reader, get hold of that dissertation: it's worth a search.

Gorran Parish Council have resolved to add the Olivers' names to the plaque on the wall in St. Goran Church, and they are determined that it shall be done in an appropriate manner.

It is anticipated that the unveiling ceremony will take place on Remembrance Sunday, 1998.

Lives of great men all remind us
We can make our lives sublime,
And departing, leave behind us
Footprints on the sands of time
                    (Longfellow)

LANHYDROCK AND THE NATIONAL TRUST

Lanhydrock is known as one of the National Trust's gems. An ineffable serenity and tranquillity seems to pervade every part of it but the background of its acquisition by the National Trust is a story of untold sadness and tragedy. Indeed, the Trust's booklet on Lanhydrock House underlines this in one of the most significant sentences within it:- 'The First World War had an even more devastating effect on the family than the Civil War'.

Read the family's involvement on the side of the Parliamentarians during the Civil War and the impact of that sentence is apparent.

The main reason was that 'Tommy' Robartes, heir to the 6th Viscount Clifden, was killed at the Battle of Loos in September, 1915. This was compounded by the terrible effects of war service on his three other brothers, Victor, Cecil and Alexander. Victor, wounded three times, was awarded the Military Cross for conspicuous gallantry. Alexander, who also received the Military Cross was equally heroic but never recovered from his injuries while Cecil's health was forever ruined by his experiences in the Rifle Brigade.

But the story of 'Tommy' Captain The Hon. Thomas Charles Reginald Agar-Robartes, named after his father when he was born in 1880, is rarely if ever mentioned.

He was undoubtedly a charismatic character and those who knew him - friends, employees and acquaintances alike - never ceased to cherish his memory. Elected an M.P. for Bodmin, his political career was brief and controversial. He was unseated in 1906 for holding a fête at Lanhydrock for party workers, although undoubtedly this breach was but a manifestation of this kindly and spirited man. However, he was returned as M.P. for St. Austell in 1908, a seat he held when war broke out in 1914, and there the tragedies of the Robartes family began.

It came as no surprise to anyone when 'Tommy' responded to

Kitchener's call, "Your country needs you". He enlisted in the Buckinghamshire Yeomanry (Royal Bucks Hussars) on 29th September, 1914, but life with a regiment in training was not for him. He sought a transfer to the Coldstream Guards and this was granted. On 5th January, 1915, Captain The Hon. T.C.R. Robartes M.P. was transferred to the 1st Battalion, Coldstream Guards at Windsor. On 3rd February his battalion, now part of the British Expeditionary Force, was moved to France.

The Allied plan was to build up and prepare for a major offensive that September. Capt. Robartes' No. 1 Coy. was stationed near St. Omer and underwent rigorous training which was termed 'not unpleasant'. On September 13th he went on "special leave (Parliamentary Duties)" and returned to his unit on 23rd September 1915. He never visited England again.

On September 19th all leave was stopped and everyone was ordered to rejoin his unit. On the 22nd the order was given for the Brigade to march eastwards to the front. The entry in the Guards' war diary for the 23rd states, 'A most unpleasant march, pouring with rain and behind the Grenadiers who have not yet learnt to keep their transport closed up.' Their march eastwards was hampered by 'the amount of troops, artillery and cavalry on the road'. Little did they realise as they marched past Allouagne that just below them was a plot of ground about ten acres in area which had been purchased in the Spring as a cemetery for those who were to be killed in the September push, but Lapugnoy military cemetery awaited them.

On 27th September the battalion marched off to occupy the 1st and 2nd lines of German trenches with orders to attack at 4.00 p.m., the woods and chalkpit on the Lens-Labassee road to support the Irish Guards. The woods and chalkpit were captured by No. 1 and No. 2 coys. who dug in on the far side. The following extract from the Coldstream Guards' war diaries is a masterpiece of understatements:-

"Many wounded men who had been out since 25th (two days earlier) were brought in. Wood and chalkpit made a very prominent salient which rendered it a difficult position to hold. At 3.45 ordered to attack .... they were shot down almost before they had got out of their trenches by a terrific machine - gun fire which enfiladed them from 3 sites. They were absolutely mown down...... the men behaved absolutely splendidly as not only were they subjected to this enormous enfilade machine-gun fire but also to a terrific bombardment by 8" shells".

Among the casualties was Tommy Robartes who, severely wounded by machine-gun fire was taken to a field dressing station where he died on 30th September. Nine other officers also died that day. He was buried at Lapugnoy Military Cemetery which he had marched past a week earlier.

The actual incident which resulted in his death is recorded officially in stark terms:-

> *'At about 6 a.m. on September 26th, 1915 - two Sergeants, Hopkins and Printer who were in this officer's company, went out in front of our trenches at the chalk pit almost up to the Bois Huge to bring in a wounded man. When they were about to return Sgt. Hopkins was shot down by a German sniper. Sgt. Printer continued on with the wounded man and brought him into the lines. Captain Robartes, who had been watching the whole episode, at once went out with Sgt. Printer and brought back Sgt. Hopkins who was severely wounded. The whole ground in front of the chalk pit was covered by the Enemy's machine guns. Captain Robartes was himself severely wounded afterwards.'*

Recommended for the V.C. for conspicuous gallantry in the field on the 28th September by Captain E.G.B. Gregge Hopwood, D.S.O.

Recommendation was dismissed.

Recommended for a high Military decoration by the Major General Commanding.

Mentioned in Despatches.

Captain Robartes' mother was inconsolable at the news of his death. When in 1923 the then Imperial War Graves Commission replaced the rough wooden crosses on the soldiers' graves with permanent headstones, she had her son's cross brought back to Lanhydrock where it lies to this day on open ground a few paces South of the church.

Tommy's grave faces a bluebell wood outside the village of Lapugnoy, five miles west of Bethune. In the Register of Graves is the following entry:-

AGAR-ROBARTES CAPT. THE HON. THOMAS CHARLES REGINALD M.P., MENTIONED IN DESPATCHES. COMMANDING NO. 2 COY., 1ST BATTALION COLDSTREAM GUARDS. DIED OF WOUNDS 30TH SEPT., 1915. ELDEST SON OF THOMAS CHARLES, 6TH VISCOUNT CLIFDEN, OF LANHYDROCK, BODMIN, CORNWALL. EDUCATED AT ETON AND CHRIST CHURCH, OXFORD. MEMBER OF PARLIAMENT FOR MID-CORNWALL.

This poignant story, typical of so many of its kind, was summed up in the poem, "ENGLAND TO HER SONS", by LIEUT. NOEL HODGSON, M.C., Devon Regt., who was killed on the first day of the Battle of the Somme, 1st July, 1916.

1. *Sons of mine, I hear you thrilling*
   To the trumpet call of war;
   Gird ye then, I give you freely
   As I gave your sires before,
   All the noblest of the children I in love and anguish bore.

2. *Free in service, wise in justice,*
   Fearing but dishonour's breath;
   Steeled to suffer uncomplaining
   Loss and failure, pain and death;
   Strong in faith that sees the issue and in hope that triumpheth.

3. *Go and may the God of battles*
   You in His good guidance keep;
   And if He in wisdom giveth
   Unto His beloved, sleep,
   I accept it nothing asking, save a little space to weep.

We will never forget the Robartes' family whose loss is our gain.

N.B. I have lodged the papers of this research with the National Trust.

*'Theirs not to make reply,
Theirs not to reason why,
Theirs but to do and die.'*
(Tennyson)

DO NOT STAND AT MY GRAVE AND WEEP

When I was searching for the grave of a Gorran man killed on the Somme in 1917 and buried in a cemetery near Bapaume, I opened the Register of Graves in which the row and number of every soldier is listed, and on the first page was the following poem:

*'Do not stand at my grave and weep
I am not there, I do not sleep.
I am the thousand winds that blow,
I am the diamond glints on snow,
I am the sunlight on ripened grain,
I am the gentle autumn rain.*

*When you awaken in the morning's hush,
I am the swift uplifted rush of birds in circling flight,
I am the soft stars that shine at night,
Do not stand at my grave and cry,
I am not there, I did not die.'*

I had never seen it in any other Register, nor in fact, had I come across it before but it was haunting. The author was not mentioned but the sentiments reminded me of Longfellow and the Story of Hiawatha: it had a Red Indian flavour. But no, it was not a Longfellow poem and a newspaper printed my request for information. I had numerous answers naming authors in some cases, but most said it was adapted from a North American Indian poem as they are Pantheists.

Some weeks later, I received from relatives in the United States a funeral card of a deceased member of the family. At the foot was this poem but there was an added line:

'I am with the risen Lord.'

But again, there was no author mentioned. I wrote to enquire as to whether or not the author was known. The reply a few weeks later was that none had been named, but the Carnegie Library in Pittsburgh had put out a request on the Internet.

Answers came from several sources but all were the same:

'There have been many claims to authorship as well as many adaptations', but the definitive answer was 'Authorship uncertain.'

The poem, though it strikes a chord somewhere in me, is unfinished and in reality meaningless. But add the line, "I am with the risen Lord," and the rest is crowned with peace, hope and eternity.

Curiously - or was it? - in my search through Longfellow's poems, I found his answer to the pagan thoughts. The lines are from his 'A Psalm of Life'.

'Dust thou art, to dust returnest,
Was not spoken of the soul.'

'Those terrible marks of the beast to the truly genteel' (Thomas Hardy)

GLOSSARY OF DIALECT WORDS USED IN GORRAN PARISH

It is often difficult for those of us who were brought up in dialect-speaking circles such as Gorran Haven to determine whether they were local dialect or the King's English. It was also true of similes and metaphors.

The following are words in daily use throughout my youth but the list is far from extensive.

abroad (adv.)   open, as in 'his mouth is always abroad'; gone fat, "She's hayved abroad this past year".

anguish (n)   inflammation: a word which is usually said in a sympathetic tone.

ballyrag (v)   to abuse, usually spoken with abuse as in "She's been busing and ballyragging all day".

beauty (n)   A fine example; a very attractive woman but rarely in this context. "She's a beauty", is more likely to mean that she is a bit 'wild and loose'.

belong (v)   to belong means the place where you live. "I belong down Mevagissey".

boiling (v)   boiling could be very hot e.g. "I'm boiling," or swarming in number, "Pilchards are boiling out in the bay."

catchpit (n)   A place, in a home usually, which was used to store things in, but evokes untidiness.

cheeld (n)   Usually used instead of girl e.g. "Is it a boy or a cheeld?" when enquiring the sex of a baby.

cluck (adj)   broody, "I'm looking for a cluck hen to put to sit."

cackylate (v) to calculate: said with pride, "I cackylate....".

cut up (v) this describes the speech of a dialect speaker who decides to speak English without a Cornish accent. "She's cutting up now that she's been away".

dagging (v) longing, desperately anxious. "I'm dagging to git home".

dishywasher (n) a pied wagtail.

evil (n) a fork with four or five prongs which are curved.

fitcher (n) a polecat but usually used in the simile "As wild as a fitcher", - in a temper.

flink (v) to flick as in, "He's flinking ink," or used to describe a woman who tosses her head in a haughty or ill-tempered way.

foreright (adj) impulsive; at the forefront always.

frizz (v) The wind may be said to be frizzing if it disturbs the water's surface, so strong: also to sizzle - "that bacon is frizzing away in the pan".

gaddle (v) to drink frequently but not normally in large quaffs. "They two do like to sit down all morning and gaddle tea, and gossip".

grafted (adv.) really dirty; a person who has not washed for a long time would be grafted.

grizzle (v) a kind of grin, sometime associated with a touch of impertinence.

helling (n) the roof - "He's up on the helling seeing to the slates".

hinderment (n)   a corruption of hindrance and widely used.

kisky   the hollow dry stem of a plant, especially hemlock

leak (n)   usually in the context of 'a little more', especially tea. "A leak more please".

lerrups   rags and tatters.

new vang (n)   a novelty of some kind; an innovation, a new practice or pastime.

nestle-bird (n)   the last of the brood whether it be person, pig or bird.

op (n)   an ope way, "He've gone up Shilly-alley-op."

pumpship (v)   to urinate, make water.

randicle (n)   a long-winded, complicated story.

ream (n)   the top of the milk which has settled (not the cream which is the real scalded or clotted cream) or the surface of the sea, "The pilchards are all up on the ream".

rora-tory (adj)   brash coloured, 'colours not seemly'.

sclow (v)   a lovely word to describe a cat scratching your hand or leg as it tries to escape: not just scratching, but digging in the claws.

sperticle (n)   a naughty, mischievous little boy, a sperticle.

stroil (n)   couch grass roots, the curse of allotment holders.

tatie (n)   potato.

ugly (adj)   foul tempered, angry. "He's in an ugly mood today".

varmint   an ill-tempered woman, and nasty as well.

wranny (n)   a wren.

Wisht, scat and zackly are well known dialect words which need no description here. But there is no English equivalent to the nuances which surround these words.